UNDERSTANDING THE U.K.

UNDERSTANDING THE U.K.

A Short Guide to British Culture, Politics, Geography, Economics and History

Henry G. Weisser *1935-*

HIPPOCRENE BOOKS
New York

For information, address: Hippocrene Books, Inc.
171 Madison Avenue, New York, NY 10016

Library of Congress Cataloging-in-Publication Data

Weisser, Henry, 1935-
    Understanding the U.K.

        Includes index.
        1. Great Britain — Civilization — 20th century.
2. Great Britain — Description and travel — 1971-
I. Title
DA566.4.W37   1987   941   87-103
ISBN 0-87052-299-X
ISBN 0-87052-428-3 (pbk.)

Printed in the United States of America.

To all those I took on tours of Britain

CONTENTS

MAPS

A WORD OF THANKS

It is impossible to name and thank all of the people who have contributed to this book through their conversations, thoughts, experiences and suggestions.

On the other hand, it is fitting to acknowledge the time and effort that two persons put into the preparation of this study. Ms. Debbie Clifford, secretary of the Colorado State University History Department, typed and edited the final draft of the manuscript. All of her work on it was accomplished with speed, efficiency, skill and remarkable pleasantness.

I must also thank my daughter, Jeanette Weisser, who is an undergraduate at the University of Colorado. Originally I recruited her to proofread my penultimate draft for such things as spelling errors and typos. To my annoyance, she brought up several questions about the clarity and content of what I had written. I soon realized that in nearly every instance her sense of the language was acute. Thereafter she collaborated as an editor as well as a proofreader, despite her busy schedule.

The history department and the central administration of Colorado State University have generously supported this project.

INTRODUCTION

This is a book for people who will go to Britain or who have been to Britain or for Anglophiles in general. It is for those who do not want to be teased by something short and superficial nor exhausted by the task of plowing through several volumes, some of them quite thick, when dealing with any of the topics in my subtitle.

Understanding the U.K. grew out of many experiences, including twenty-seven years of studying the subject and twenty-four years of teaching it. For many years, I have been the person directly responsible for explaining British civilization at a large western university, Colorado State University, where I am a professor of history. All during this time, people came to me with questions such as: "Does the Queen have any real power? What are British universities really like? What is 'shepherd's pie'? What are the best places to visit if you only have one week in England?" I hope that this book answers all of these questions and hundreds more.

I lived in Britain on several occasions, and I have crossed the Atlantic a total of twenty-four times so far. Over the years, I have had discussions on all kinds of subjects with diverse and varied British people. Yet the most informative insights for many sections of this book came from conducting six student tours to the U.K. and Ireland. I was able to share in the excitement of well over a hundred people who were exploring Britain for the first time. *Understanding the U.K.* contains the kind of information they needed to know to get the most out of their visit.

This book should have other uses besides preparing visitors to the U.K. People who have returned might want to read it in order to reflect about what they heard and saw. Those involved with Britain for a long time themselves might find reading some sections entertaining. Anyone involved in Anglo-American relationships might get some insights from it. It also ought to be useful for those who plan to spend six months or a year in Britain on sabbatical or for business purposes. It can also serve as an introduction to Britain for college survey classes.

The author expects criticism for being opinionated, idiosyncratic, for shooting from the hip, creating stereotypes and offering generalizations that are too sweeping. Such must be the price of attempting to present an account of a civilization that stretches back over two thousand years and is represented by over fifty-five million live and diverse inhabitants. What I can say in defense is that I have tried to be careful and balanced throughout and to rely upon a wide variety of sources, living and printed. I hope that the usefulness of this treatment will outweigh criticisms that readers may find.

One final thought. Nearly everything in these pages has been written with a firm conviction that one of the best things any American can do to enhance life is to spend some time in Britain.

CHAPTER ONE

Some Practical Considerations

HOW TO DEAL WITH ANGLO-AMERICAN CULTURE SHOCK

What Is it?

Despite a common language, a partially shared history and a similar philosophical outlook on the most important subjects in life, the two main branches of English-speaking culture on either side of the Atlantic Ocean have been diverging somewhat for hundreds of years. The American visitor to Britain is confronted with a plethora of details that are different from the details at home. Culture shock is the cumulative effect of these differences. The details can be material, in the form of plugs with strange prongs, kettles with strange switches, curious heating devices or doors that open inwardly when they are expected to swing out-

3

wards. Some details take the form of strange words and phrases that need translation, such as "white tea" or "p" or "V.A.T." or strange usage, such as references to Europe as some other place than Britain itself. Some details involve the clock; there are odd times to do banking, shopping and drinking. There are odd holidays. Then there are behavioral customs and practices that are different. For example, the check-out clerk at a grocery store will not bag purchases gleefully or have anyone else do it. Behind all these details are larger patterns of social behavior and human interaction that produce a much more subtle and pervasive form of culture shock. Taken together, the effect of all of these differences can, at worst, leave the visitor frazzled, dazed, frustrated, exhausted and withdrawn all at once.

British Characteristics to Look For

Educated persons everywhere know how damaging stereotypes can be and how a great variety of humans and human behaviors exists in any population category. Even so, some behaviors show up with sufficient frequency in Britain to be labeled national characteristics. Of course, some Britons will have none of them, but most are likely to carry on with at least some of them. It will be helpful for the prospective American visitor to know something about these national characteristics in order to minimize the effect of culture shock.

Politeness
Americans in Britain will tend to be polite, but in their own informal, folksy and breezy manner. British politeness is different. It has a ritualized predictability, an expected formality.

While Americans will often hold doors open for people following, they will not do it in the prescribed, ritualized British manner. This includes automatically casting a glance over the shoulder to see who is coming next, holding the door like a machine and primly acknowledging the "thank you" from the next person with a nod or a smile.

In Britain, "please" and "thank you" are involved in just about every human transaction. These words are spoken automatically, sharply and without hesitation. They are normal, necessary and expected parts of the sentences involved. Sometimes there are elaborations, such as "thank you very much indeed." Americans appear at their worst when they say such things as "Give me . . ." or "Would you let me have . . ." or "I'd like . . ." or "I want . . . ." Omitting "please" immediately labels the American as a boor, a label confirmed when "thank you" or "thank you very much" is omitted at the time goods or services are supplied.

People in the north of England tend to be less formal than their southern counterparts. They are apt to say "ta" for thank you, which is similar to the American "thanks." Curiously, British people do not say "you are welcome." Instead, another "thank you" might take its place.

There is a way of preparing for this aspect of British politeness. Practice aloud saying a clear "please" for everything and a clear, articulated "thank you" for everything. Have someone close pay attention to your efforts who is prepared to signal with a nudge when you forget. When in Britain, observe how the British do it and follow suit.

Sacred Queues
American visitors in Britain are likely to spend

much more time standing in long lines, which are called "queues" in Britain, which is identical to the French word for tail and is pronounced "cue." Long lines indicate Britain's crowded condition. It is possible, for example, to have up to twenty-five people queued up in the fast lane of a store belonging to the most modern supermarket chain in Britain. Moreover, the ordinary neighborhood butcher shop in the high (main) street can have long lines stretching out to the sidewalk on a Saturday morning.

The queues are sacred. They stand for fairness, justice, discipline and order — the very best that British civilization has ever offered — so woe to the American who is too casual about his place on one of them. British queues form quickly and naturally. They are noted for being peaceful, straight and disciplined. Everyone seems to know where his or her place is and where everyone else's is as well. The mob scenes of pushing, shouting, shoving to the front and milling about in many Continental countries and in many Third World countries hardly every happen in Britain. Compared to the Italians and the French, Americans do form orderly lines fairly well, but not nearly as well as the British do. The occasional American visitor who aggressively tries to slip towards the front may hear the mutter "bloody Yank" coming from the long, patient line.

Precision in Language Use

In Britain, very high value is placed upon how the language is used, and many Americans soon come to the realization that, up against good British conversationalists, their pronunciation is comparatively sloppy, their vocabulary underdeveloped and their verbal agility inadequate. All of this can be intimidating for

Americans, but it is much more so for less articulate Britons themselves because it is in the realm of language that their class, educational background and status are starkly revealed.

Americans who are in Britain for a long time discover that their enunciation becomes clearer and more distinct. American tendencies to slur the ends of words or to drop final "g" participles are overcome. In time, Americans are likely to put out more effort in constructing lucid and artful sentences. Of course, this can be carried to extremes of imitation, as when the American "a" becomes the British "a." Somehow, Americans who abandon all of their native sounds seem somewhat phony.

Improvements in American speech in Britain occur in large measure because speaking well is so obviously highly regarded in Britain, to the extent of being treasured as an art by educated persons. Visitors who can express themselves well in standard English are always esteemed, no matter what foreign national accent they may have, "broad American" or any other.

Shouting Is Shunned

If the American visitor shouts in an argument with a British person, he loses the argument virtually automatically. Shouters are perceived as those persons who have failed to handle the intellectual content of a disagreement and must raise their voices in order to compensate for their dim intelligence. This attitude is difficult for many Americans to deal with because they have been raised with examples of heroic shouters, such as John Wayne, who raise their voices when something callous, unfair, cruel or dishonest has been perpetrated. Yet shouting in Britain produces counter-productive reactions; the more the American shouts, the more smug the Briton becomes. The Briton knows that he or she has won at that point, although victory might be signaled only by the lowering of the head to repress a flickering smile or by dumb resignation at having to deal with a barbarian.

In a classic Anglo-American exchange, a Briton might warn: "You are shouting!" which might bring on the all-American riposte: "There is something to shout about!"

The way for an American to engage in a dispute in Britain on an equal footing is, first of all, to lower one's voice and keep it low throughout the argument. Second, stick to the facts exclusively. Never go to an *ad hominem* argument, that is, an argument that attacks or puts down the opponent personally. In general, well-educated British people argue in this fashion, with lowered voices taking up the facts precisely. Yet there are less than polite Britons, such as irate bus drivers who will, when exasperated, shout at Americans. The thing to do in such circumstances is not to respond in kind. Instead, keep your voice low and stick to the facts! This method, by the way, can even be effective in the United States!

Reserve

A perceptive Czech once observed that people from the Continent give themselves an air of importance by talking, while an Englishman does so by holding his tongue. This reserve carries over into social situations, and it has inspired many ethnic jokes about the English. English people newly introduced to one another sometimes sit on the edge of their chairs in painful awkwardness while they earnestly cast about for a safe, impersonal subject to discuss. They usually hit upon the weather.

Breezily open Americans act differently. Give an American a chair and a drink, and in ten minutes he or she will be in the midst of important aspects of one's life history. British people usually have to know one another for a time before allowing exchanges about their backgrounds, or about the strengths and weaknesses operating in their lives.

The class system of Britain may play an important role in reinforcing social reserve. All too often, British people are rapt players at the game of defining people in categories of class and status. Therefore, information about backgrounds and lifestyles may not be given out readily.

The openness and freeness of Americans is often appreciated by Britons in contrast to their own caution. What they often do not see is that many Americans have a deeper and hidden wall of reserve of their own, well behind their openness and smiles.

In one social circumstance the British are clearly more egalitarian and open than Americans. Older people are not so discriminated against or segregated or shunted aside or shipped away as they are in the United States. Respect for the elderly is clearly indicated by how they are spoken to without condescension by younger people. Moreover, social activities in Britain, such as dances, do not have the usual age segregation patterns that occur in the United States, where persons in one age group feel awkward if another age group is present in substantial numbers. In Britain, people of all ages seem to enjoy activities in mixed age groups.

One resolute conviction seems to have something to do with British reserve, namely the belief that despite all the problems of class and economics, they belong to the most civilized society on earth and that as individuals they are the best examples of what civilized human beings are supposed to be. The self-assured egotism of the British was once conveyed starkly to the author by a woman who declared: "If it were not for the weather, England would be the best place on earth to live because the people are the nicest one can find."

Respect for Privacy

British reserve can be considered part of an almost sacred respect for privacy that prevails. Individual space, freedom and rights are all respected. Perhaps that is why Britain has been known as the homeland of so many colorful eccentrics.

Respect for privacy is undoubtedly in large measure a response to the extremely crowded conditions found over most of the island. The number of inhabitants per square mile in England is not that far behind the figure for Japan, so heightened respect for privacy can be seen as a necessary adaptation to a situation where houses, apartments and even non-related people within apartments tend to be all crowded in upon one another. Space is a luxury in Britain.

Two aspects of life in Britain seem to contradict this respect for privacy. First, British people tend to stand much closer when talking than Americans do here. An American who asks directions of a stranger will be surprised at how close the stranger stands when providing information. Second, the fumes of British smoke seem to be everywhere, invading the privacy of lungs. Anti-smoking regulations are not as pervasive in Britain as in America, and a higher percentage of the population seems to smoke. Often the visitor can see very old people and very young people taking the last puff right down to their yellowed fingertips. That such a large number of people should smoke in Britain seems odd because tobacco is very costly, and many brands of cigarettes are of questionable quality.

Materialism

One of the frequent criticisms that some Americans make about their own society is that it is so materialistic. World travelers know that materialism is rampant throughout the world. Americans are outstanding not simply for being materialistic but in the fact that they are so good at acquiring large quantities of the coveted materials. Do not be surprised if ordinary Britons are not as interested in the local castle or cathedral as they are in how may pounds they find in their pay envelopes and in what very specific things those pounds can buy. Britons' intellectual energies are often consumed by carefully calculating what they can afford and how they can add to their possessions over time. The difference between these Britons and their American counterparts is that Americans have an easier time doing it.

The Image of Heroic Retreat

Despite their many victories over several centuries of international conflict, the British love to dwell upon those episodes when they were outnumbered and surrounded. Heroic retreats and last stands, in which courage and fortitude were displayed against staggering odds, are given special celebration. For example, the most treasured memories of World War II seem to be Dunkirk and the Blitz of London rather than the crossing of the Rhine, the reoccupation of Singapore and Hong Kong or the conquest of western Germany. Similarly, isolated colonial battalions that went down

fighting hordes of spear-throwing savages in remote
corners of the world are celebrated in paintings, songs
and stories. Maintaining cool, determined courage in a
hopeless position seems to be the very essence of
heroism for the British. Perhaps it comes from their
emphasis on the study of the ancient Greeks, who
stressed the same kind of heroic episodes. It certainly
is not the gaudy, boastful and triumphant heroism of
ancient Rome, or of Hitler or Mussolini or Red
Square.

Public Safety

Despite recent Irish terrorist violence and the
publicity given to some teenage toughs, Britain's urban environments are among the safest in the world.
Some unpopular sections of London and Glasgow may
not be safe at night, but such locales are exceptions. In
nearly all the other British towns and cities, American
visitors can feel safe at all hours. Compared with
American cities, Britain's crime rate is extremely low,
the inhabitants predictably friendly, and the police
present and efficient. So do not hesitate to go out at
any time.

Confronting Your Own Nationality in Britain:
American Characteristics to Look For

One of the best ways to comprehend the dimen-
sions of one's own nationality is to leave that nation
for a time. When Americans become totally immersed
in the British environment, they are often shocked by
revelations of their own national characteristics. Normal, natural behavior at home can suddenly become
aberrant behavior abroad. As a result, certain characteristics stand forth in stark relief as typically Ameri-

can despite the variety and diversity in American life stemming from ethnicity, regionalism and individualism.

One complication arises from the fact that many Americans have chosen to live in Britain permanently, some of whom are noted for blending into the environment rather easily. They might speak in a very British way, with lowered tones, and their manners might be noteworthy for impersonal understatement. Many of these expatriate Americans have an East Coast background featuring a high level of education, and they are likely to be professionals. American visitors might not even be able to identify them as fellow countrymen.

The British are, of course, quite used to them, and they are also very used to the Americans who stand out glaringly as such because floods of American tourists have poured into Britain regularly for decades. The British know what to look for and what to expect as American characteristics. Most of the Americans who have never been abroad, on the other hand, will probably be seeing them in stark relief for the first time.

Loudness

The first and foremost American characteristic is loudness. Americans seem so much louder in Britain than they do at home. They can be heard coming a mile away. They shout to each other across open, public spaces, which is something Britons ordinarily do not do. Americans seem to be bellowing, howling and gesticulating everywhere. They can even be heard roaring over the rattles and crashes in cheap British cafés.

Of course, there are millions of quiet Americans who would not be noticed for their volume in Britain or anywhere. But a trip to Britain will prove that there is no silent majority among tourists.

To be sure, tourists are likely to have high spirits from the fact that they are on vacation. Even so, British people who are polite will make a point of always approaching a person closely before speaking. What could be more American, with the possible exception of apple pie, than a loud shout echoing down twenty-five yards of an historic British street: "Hey! Did you see this over here?"

British shouters exist also, but they are immediately dismissed as the ill-bred, ill-mannered and ill-educated. If they are young enough, they earn the label "young louts."

American Clothes and Americans Wearing British Clothes

Loud clothes are another indication of the American presence. Americans can be spotted at a considerable distance along a crowded British thoroughfare by the bright colors they wear, often in strange combinations. Americans don ski style clothes for travel in winter and California style, casual clothes for travel in summer. American parkas, hiking shoes, T-shirts and shorts are dead giveaways of their nationality.

As a rule, British people tend to dress in a more staid and sober manner, wearing more high quality, well-tailored items than Americans do. Across the board, they tend to have fewer but better items of apparel. Consequently, the ups and downs of fashion have less of an impact for most Britons. Britain is certainly much less a throw-away society when it comes to clothes. In fact, in most long queues one can usually spot at least a few "old dears," or older ladies, who tend to sport hats and coats that look as if they are well preserved from the days of World War II.

Many Americans rush to buy and wear British clothes when they get there, since tweeds, sweaters and other well-made items comprise some of the best bargains that the country has to offer. Yet even wearing British clothes, Americans still present some contrasts. An American man will often sport his Harris tweed jacket at occasions when considerable dress is required. His British counterpart will tend to wear a very good, conservative suit instead, and take his Harris tweed for a weekend in the country or to a sports event. After all, these are the occasions for which these wonderful coats were designed. (By the way, they seem to last forever.)

Young Americans rush to buy and wear the latest *avant garde* British fashions whether they go to Britain or purchase them at home. In this field since World War II, Britain has come up with some startling innovations. After all, the mini-skirt, Mary Quant, the designer, and Twiggy, the thin model, were all part of the pop culture that roared out of Carnaby Street not too long ago. Colorful pop fashions, daring and innovative, continue to blossom in Britain. Fairly recently, the "mod" style turned heads, and most recently many American high school students have taken up "punk" styles, featuring dyed and radically shaved hair, metal studded wrist bands and collars and many items made of leather.

Even among the popular fads of youth, there are differences between how the British and Americans utilize them. British youngsters will tend to wear the fashionable items long before their style penetrates to the interior of the United States. By the time Americans from Iowa or Idaho take them up, British youth will be on to something else.

Another difference is that in America the affluent young suburbanites with disposable income are likely to take up the latest popular British fashion. Most of these enthusiasts plan to go to college and pursue high-paying careers. By contrast, the very innovators of these styles in Britain are the young people who have nowhere to go. These are the people whose educations come to an early end and whose work lives begin at some boring or unpleasant jobs that have no future. The shocking, new, daring, colorful and often outrageous styles are their way of making a statement in life, which is something they cannot do in any other sphere. It may be all that they have going for them. Such young Britons are not likely to feel that they have much in common with those affluent and upwardly mobile young Americans who seek to imitate their exterior images.

Pragmatism, Speed and Efficiency

In Britain, Americans have the reputation of being the world's foremost pragmatists, which means, roughly, that they are the most keenly interested in having things work. Americans want to solve problems, get answers and get whatever needs to be done accomplished. Spiritual, philosophical and aesthetic considerations are not their central focus.

Americans are also noted for demanding speed and efficiency from themselves and from people of other nationalities. They want things done without delay and with predictability.

Almost everywhere in Britain, these pragmatic Americans who live by the clock find themselves frustrated by slowness and inefficiency. Many things are accomplished only after maddening delays, and other things are done in the most roundabout manner.

There are two ironies here. In the Victorian era, the British themselves were the foremost pragmatists of the world, similarly noted for their speed and efficiency. At that time, American life was still basically agrarian, and the United States imported efficiently earned British capital. Another irony is that the British exhibit the same impatience and bewilderment when they deal with the Irish, which is an old story.

One example involving road repairs can serve to show how the American who takes speed and efficiency for granted can be in for culture shock in Britain. When Americans decide to fix a road intersection by widening it, they are likely to send in a fleet of trucks and equipment and a small army of workers. After a short period of time engulfed in tar, noise and confusion, they will transform the intersection and move on elsewhere. A typical British operation at an intersection will involve fewer people, and smaller and fewer pieces of equipment. What is truly remarkable, though, is that the process seems to drag on forever. The roadworkers are called "navvies," a carryover from the time when they built railroads, and they seem to slog on at their own sweet pace. For example, when a board is needed from a distant pile, one man goes to fetch it, slowly and deliberately, and carries it back even more slowly and deliberately. He is not likely to do it alone because someone will saunter along with him, perhaps to make sure that he picks up the right board, or to make sure that it is balanced securely on his shoulder, or, most likely, just to take a break.

At one such seemingly never-ending road repair site, the author, who regularly passed by it on foot, asked in March whether they planned to finish off the project in July. After a long pause and a searching glance heavenward, a navvy answered in the most innocent and gentle of all Irish brogues, "Which July?"

Cleanliness

Another American characteristic is the demand for a high degree of cleanliness, something that is not sufficiently available in most of Britain and even less so in many other parts of Europe. In Britain, the American preoccupation with cleanliness is perceived as an obsession as they daily shower, shampoo and splash chemicals on. Britons are often amused at what they see as a fetish of cleanliness. For example, the reassuring messages about sanitation inscribed on the paper bands put around toilet seats in American motels are likely to provoke strong laughter from Britons unaccustomed to them. Americans, on the other hand, are not amused at the lower standards of cleanliness they find throughout Britain. Americans in the cheaper British hotels have one of the worst manifestations of culture shock when they discover that they either have to take tub baths or wash themselves at a sink. Some of them exhibit the peeved reaction that can be called a shower withdrawal syndrome.

Boastful Affluence

The Americans who are so clean and so loud in Britain are from the ranks of the affluent, with relatively few exceptions. After all, the poor and the struggling have to stay at home trying to make ends meet, unless they are adventurous students who go to Britain on a shoestring.

Thanks to the old images from Hollywood and the new images from TV serials, Britons expect Americans to be affluent. Raw statistics on per capita income do show Americans considerably ahead of their British counterparts, although both nationalities are certainly far ahead of most of the world when it comes to commanding goods and services.

Even so, the disparity between British and American affluence is exaggerated by the fact that financially comfortable Americans in Britain display a penchant for boasting about size. Americans tend to go on about how much larger all sorts of things are at home when compared to similar items in Britain. Americans make frequent invidious comparisons about cars, refrigerators, TV sets, apartments, bathrooms, kitchens, gardens and yards. Americans also boast about the size of farms, parks, the number of doctors available and the number of students at various universities. The message is painfully clear: bigger is supposed to mean better.

British people share the blame for this boasting because some do ask visitors to make comparisons about the size of their refrigerator or car or kitchen with similar items back in America. Perhaps they do this because it provides a topic guaranteed to generate American enthusiasm and animation.

Naturally, the most enthusiastic and animated of Americans are the Texans. The British have a particular fascination with them. The stereotype of the Texan as a particularly loud and exceedingly boastful individual who behaves in an outrageously familiar and friendly manner is often highly esteemed in Britain. Perhaps this is because the Texan carries some American characteristics to their most extreme manifestation. The British love to have Texans almost lose control of themselves as they describe how huge and wonderful and spectacular things are in the second largest state in the Union. Dull by comparison are the Canadians or the New Englanders who look and sound much more like the British themselves.

USING LIMITED TIME IN BRITAIN EFFECTIVELY

The number of things that can be seen and done and savored in Britain's area of less than one hundred thousand square miles is simply breathtaking. It is quite possible to go back to Britain year after year and find a new historic town, or a new ancient site, or a new stately home or a new, interesting valley each and every time. Similarly, a yearly visitor to London can find on every trip a new neighborhood, a new museum, a new spectacular sight and a new charming corner. Britain is so rich and varied in its civilization that the hapless visitor from a rather plain part of the United States must feel like a malnourished orphan suddenly set before a huge, magnificent buffet. Starving orphans in such circumstances can gorge and get sick, and so can the avid visitor who rushes about in a mad haste to encompass everything.

Everybody has to operate in this world on limited time. Yet a trip to Britain, especially if it has been looked forward to for a long time, demands that much activity must be pushed into a short time frame of perhaps one to three weeks. How is it possible to get everything seen and done in so short a time? Reality demands that limitations must be imposed. Shortcuts need to be considered.

A Shortcut: Seeking Your Own Special Quest

Nearly everyone who goes to Britain has some special personal quest. It may not be a classic tourist attraction. The quest may come from a childhood dream, an adolescent longing or an adult fantasy.

Whatever it is, this special quest should not be

squeezed into a long list of obligatory things to see and do. Instead, it should be given a whole chunk of precious time and treated as a top priority. Everyone should try to experience the reality of that which is sought after.

The nature of such special quests in Britain varies from person to person, and what might seem extraordinarily special to one individual might seem insignificant or even silly to another. Such is the variety of human responses. But you must dare to do what might seem silly to others.

The author indulged himself on his own special quest many years ago. It consisted of going to Lyme Regis on the south coast of England to seek out the scenes of John Fowles' novel, *The French Lieutenant's Woman*, long before these places had become famous in America through the film. Indeed, I looked for the fictitious Sarah out on the ocean causeway, and saw the rough hillsides where she walked. Viewed objectively, this was a silly thing for an historian to do with very limited time available for a research project that had to be carried out in the libraries of London. Why should I look for the scenes of an English novel when I do not teach English literature? Yet it was important for me.

I have seen many other Americans take off on similar private, personal side trips. One young American had always wanted to ride a horse in a London park. It made no difference that her trip to Britain occurred in mid-winter. In foul weather, London stables ordinarily do not rent out their horses. Nevertheless, she persisted, and on one fair day she got her horse from one stable that was so far from a park that she had to ride her steed through dense and frightening London traffic before she reached the park's paths.

Yet I did not have to ask her whether the time, expense and trouble were worth it because her face gave the answer.

Another acquaintance just had to see James Herriot's Yorkshire, and, if she could, observe the famous veterinarian himself. I saw a whole troop of young Americans go off to Liverpool to worship at the shrines of the Beatles. Until this rock group came along, no one would ever think of tourists making a pilgrimage to busy, grim but friendly Liverpool. Others have made pilgrimages on the underground railway of London out to the grave of Karl Marx in rather nondescript Highgate Cemetery. More romantic visitors have chased the memory of King Arthur in the west of England, at places such as Glastonbury. There are also some Richard III buffs who firmly believe that Shakespeare's villain was one of the most unfairly maligned figures in all of history. These people spend time in York because Richard spent so much of his time there. Then there are those people who go down to Portsmouth to walk the deck of the flagship of their hero, Horatio Nelson. His ship, the *Victory,* is beautifully preserved at a magnificent maritime museum.

A special quest for a surprising number of Americans is one of Britain's most famous attractions—Stonehenge. Americans can be seen flocking around the great prehistoric stone circle at any time of the year. If Stonehenge is very special for you for whatever reasons, occult or otherwise, be sure to get out to Salisbury plain to see it.

These are just a few examples of the kinds of things that Americans have made a point of seeing on their own special quest in Britain. Yours may be one of these, or something entirely different, or you may not be conscious of one at this stage. But if you have a special quest in mind, and have a chance to do it, it is well worth the time and effort, even if you must cut other things from your itinerary. You will never forget achieving it, long after some of the other things seen on the trip become dim recollections or fade entirely.

Other Shortcuts: Thinking in Categories

Another way of handling a limited amount of time to deal with Britain's fabulous abundance of things to see is to think of categories. There are just too many castles, cathedrals, museums, galleries, great houses, palaces, medieval towns, historic cities, seaports and absolute "musts" in London. Life is hardly long enough to see all of them, let alone a two- or three-week sojourn. Even so, a short stay can allow a visit to a good example or a couple of examples in each of these categories. For instance, if the visitor is able to get to and appreciate one magnificent Welsh castle, he or she can return to the United States happy with memories of that experience even if there are a dozen more in the vicinity that were bypassed. Return trips can be planned to see some of the others at other times.

What follows are some specific suggestions for things to see in Britain when time is limited. They are arranged in convenient categories and are drawn from the experiences of many visitors over many years. The secret of all of this is to experience at least one exciting possibility from each category.

Castles
There is no more delightful castle than Conway, set in the magnificent scenery of northwest Wales. It stands partly in ruins and can be explored thoroughly,

to the extent of climbing the tallest turrets. Mountains, the sea and a completely walled small town contribute to make this place a breathtaking delight. Visitors from Colorado, hardly strangers to natural beauty, have become simply enchanted with the beauty of Conway.

In England, Warwick Castle (one should not pronounce the second *w*), close to Stratford-upon-Avon, is grand, although in recent years it has become rather commercialized.

Among other castles, Harlech and Carnarvon in Wales are impressive. Various other castles are distributed all over Britain, in conditions varying from ruins to regularly occupied castles redone as family mansions or hotels.

There is more commentary on castles in the chapter on history.

Cathedrals

There are many gorgeous cathedrals to choose from, each so unique that there can be no answer to the question of which one is the best to see. Canterbury, Lincoln, Durham, Wells and Salisbury are all among the more spectacular. Coventry should be mentioned as well because it has a noted twentieth century cathedral joined to the bombed-out shell of the old medieval edifice.

Since these ancient buildings need constant repairs, it is unlikely that the visitor will come upon them without scaffolding obscuring part of them. Be sure to make a generous voluntary contribution whenever you go into a cathedral to help facilitate this work. These buildings really belong to all of us, and they certainly ought to belong to future generations as well.

Most cathedrals have information phones installed at key locations. The messages heard over them tend to be extremely detailed, so the specialized vocabulary for cathedrals presented in the chapter on history should be useful.

A number of lesser church functionaries are likely to be drifting about, presumably keeping an eye on things. They can become a fund of information. Do not hesitate to question them because in most cases they will be happy to respond in full.

Ancient Universities

Here is the choice is simple — either Oxford or Cambridge. Most of the other universities of Britain are of much more recent origin, as attested to by the red brick or the aluminum and glass materials of their buildings.

Both universities are in magnificent towns. Oxford University is close to London, in the midst of a crowded, bustling commercial and light manufacturing center. Cambridge is more remote and quieter.

To see either one of these universities go first to the tourist information center and then, armed with guidebooks and pamphlets, go on a long prowl inside and outside of the buildings. There will be some quadrangles and buildings off limits, but there will be many exciting places open to the public, such as chapels and famous towers that can be climbed. Each city also has several wonderful old museums.

A day spent strolling about in either Oxford or Cambridge will be highly rewarding. There is no better way of appreciating the deep roots and strikingly different appearance of traditional British education.

Museums and Art Galleries

London is the place to find world famous galleries and museums. In addition, just about every fair-sized town in Britain has its own museum and gallery worth a quick visit. One nice aspect of provincial museums and galleries is that their relatively small size does not daunt the visitor the way that the truly gigantic museums and galleries of London do.

Which of all the many wonderful museums and galleries in London should be chosen if only a limited time is available? It is pointless to rush through as many as possible on a mad, exhausting race, as too many people do. Instead, be selective according to your own individual inclinations and expertise.

The British Museum will fascinate nearly everyone because it contains a fantastically varied collection of art and artifacts from all over the world, including mummies, marbles from the Acropolis, Japanese ceramics, gorgeous illustrated books, stamp collections and priceless documents from English history.

Two world-famous art galleries are right on Trafalgar Square: the National Gallery, housing British and European paintings, and the National Portrait Gallery. Another highly important gallery, some distance to the west, is the Tate Gallery.

The Victoria and Albert Museum has a huge collection of various fine arts. The Science Museum is nearby and should not be missed by people interested in engineering. For those who have a military interest, the Imperial War Museum will be a must. Those keen on anthropology should see the Museum of Mankind. A splendid new museum has opened recently, the London Museum, which is devoted to everything about the metropolis, from the earliest times to the present. There is also a new and interesting museum devoted to the Battle of Britain. Madam Tussaud's Waxworks Museum is the most famous of its type, and always guaranteed to delight younger people.

London Sights That Must Be Seen

In addition to the British Museum, the National Gallery, the National Portrait Gallery and the Tate Gallery, all of which can be considered "musts" for any visitor, there are three other sights in London that absolutely have to be seen, even if time is short.

The Tower of London is an historic treasure on account of all of the great events and people from English history associated with it. Beefeater guards, drawn from specially selected veterans, serve as informative guides. The best way to see the Tower is on one of their lively tours, which is included in the price of admission.

Westminster Abbey is right across the way from the Houses of Parliament. At Westminster Abbey, most of Britain's illustrious dead are laid to rest, including famous kings, queens, poets and statesmen. It is possible to browse about on your own, but there are good tours available at a modest price from the guides.

Parliament should be seen, but it is sometimes difficult to get in. Long lines and long waits might impose between the visitor and the actual sessions on the floor, if they happen to be held at the time the visitor is in London. Should time be very short, see what you can by walking around outside and by getting as far as possible walking around inside, which may not be very far at all.

Another worthwhile experience is to get an overall basic orientation and a quick view of the great sights by taking the Around London Bus Tour provided by the London Transport Service. Fairly inexpensive tour buses leave Piccadilly Circus regularly.

Historic Towns and Cities

There are so many wonderful historic towns and cities to choose from that the visitor is bound to feel confused as well as certain that many important places will be missed. Indeed, it would take a lifetime of visits to come close to seeing all of them, so the best thing to do is to break them down into categories and see one place that is a worthy representative of each kind of historic urban era. These categories emerge: ancient archiepiscopal cities; ancient university towns; ancient seaports; workaday places; Scottish cities and towns; and places that are so unique they do not fit into categories.

Ancient Archiepiscopal Cities — There are only two to choose from — Canterbury and York. Each was with London one of the three most important English cities in the Middle Ages. Much of their medieval nature remains, including old streets and a magnificent cathedral in each city. Get to at least one of them.

Ancient University Towns — Again, there is a choice of one out of two, Oxford or Cambridge, and both places have already been discussed under Ancient Universities.

Cathedral Towns — Lincoln, Durham, Salisbury and Winchester are all exceptional cathedral towns because they have considerable charm in addition to their magnificent cathedrals. A trip to Salisbury will allow a quick side trip to Stonehenge. An advantage of a trip to Winchester, where the cathedral is not as imposing as others, is that Arthurian legends can be pursued there.

Ancient Seaports — The coasts of Britain have a

number of beautiful old towns that are rich in history and utterly charming because, for one reason or another, they have never had the opportunity to grow and sprawl and become modern the way their successful rival towns have. Some of them "froze" to an extent when their rivers or harbors silted up and thereby ruined their trade. They are all charming, relatively small and worth a trip. Fowey, King's Lynn and Lyme Regis are good examples. Rye deserves a special word because it is so accessible from London and so lovely. Brighton should not be on this list because it is larger and tends to evoke the nineteenth and early twentieth centuries. The other ancient seaport towns are quite able to bring the visitor back to Elizabethan times if he or she gives the imagination a little play.

Workaday Places — At least some time should be spent looking at one industrial, ordinary, grim town because such is the workaday world for the majority of Britons. These grimmer places are regularly bypassed by tourists, who steer towards "green England." Towns such as Birmingham, Liverpool, Manchester, Coventry, Newcastle-upon-Tyne and Leeds make up a substantial part of what is called "black England." Factories, workshops, railyards, coal heaps, chimneys, row houses and utilitarian shopping centers fill these urban landscapes. Several of these places can provide a worthwhile side benefit for the visitor. Coventry has a striking modern cathedral; Birmingham is the second largest city in Britain; Liverpool has some of the early haunts of the Beatles; and Manchester and Newcastle-upon-Tyne are exceptionally friendly cities.

Scottish Cities — Edinburgh is one of the most historic cities in Europe, and has its own stark beauty. It is second only to London in having a concentration of museums, art galleries and historic sites. The "Royal

Mile" is a magnificent axis for history, running from Edinburgh Castle at one end and Holyrood Palace at the other. John Knox's house and St. Giles Church are among the sites that lie in between. Edinburgh's beauty is of a slate gray color reflected by acres and acres of old buildings.

Scotland's other large urban area, Glasgow, is sad in this era because of the high rate of unemployment and consequent poverty. It is also perhaps the least safe place to be in Britain.

Scotland's smaller towns in the Highland region can be disappointing because they are mostly rather recent looking and tend to have a similar appearance. One gem is the old college town of St. Andrews, rich with its ancient ruins, old university and dedication to golf.

Bath — Bath was long known as a famous spa. Its wealthy devotees of the eighteenth century were responsible for the splendid Georgian architecture that predominates, including the two great crescents of apartment buildings. Bath's Abbey and Roman remains are other attractions of this lovely town.

Chester — Chester is located in the northwest of England and has much to offer from its rich past. There are arcades, old city walls, a cathedral, scenes that evoke the seventeenth century and Roman remains. Chester is a good town for walks.

Chipping Campden — Not far from London is a lovely area of the west Midlands once devoted to sheep farming. It is the Cotswold region, where picturesque villages sprinkle rolling hills. Chipping Campden is one of the best preserved of them, but there are many more nearby. This region is best seen by car.

Conway, Wales — This entirely walled medieval gem lies in the shadow of massive Conway castle, discussed in the section under Castles.

Stratford-upon-Avon — This town is a must for all of the passionate admirers of Shakespeare. They can see the streets where he walked, the house where he was born, the church where he is buried and the river he crossed over many times. Older inhabitants say that so many tourist buses roar into the area that it is reminiscent of the preparations for the D-Day invasion. Such popularity has had some negative effects, particularly in making Stratford a tourist town, filled with souvenirs and people jaded towards new faces. If your love for Shakespeare is ardent, do go; if not, you can skip it.

Warwick — Besides having a marvelous castle, mentioned earlier, Warwick is a charming small town, good for walking around. Delightful scenery and old buildings abound.

TRANSPORTATION

The Hapless Pedestrian

The survival of pedestrians in Britain is nothing short of an ongoing miracle. Hazards are worst in London, of course, but everywhere in Britain cars are driven with a controlled fury that places the pedestrian's life in danger. While drivers are more polite to pedestrians in Britain than they are on the Continent, drivers and pedestrians are antagonists nonetheless for space and the right of way. Given the weight of armor drivers possess, it is best for the pedestrian not to challenge them. American drivers tend to be more relaxed, gallant and considerate of pedestrians, particularly in the American West. In Britain, nine out of ten drivers have the spirit and skills, but not the vocabulary, of the typical New York City taxi driver.

There is one safe road crossing for pedestrians in Britain that is sacred. It is called the zebra, a word pronounced with a sharp double "e" in America and a flat short "e" (as the "e" in bed) in Britain. These crossings have large white stripes and flashing orange beacons on poles on either side. Cars must stop at these zones when pedestrians enter, and, amazingly, 99 percent of them do, yet another tribute to the law-abiding nature of the British. Pedestrians should be bold on a zebra because it is his or her clear right of way at all times. Enter one and be amazed at how ferocious columns of vehicles shudder to a halt in your honor. But keep a wary eye out for the driver who might belong to that one percent not likely to stop.

Sometimes extremely busy streets appear to be without zebras, making crossing an extremely risky business. Pedestrians should look around for a "subway" at such places. These are not subways in the American sense of the term. The "underground" is the equivalent term for an American "subway." A British "subway" is a convenient pedestrian underpass, found rather frequently in British cities. Foreign pedestrians often miss them and then become frustrated at the numerous iron fences that seem to thwart access to intersections but actually function to channel the flow of pedestrians away from tempting but dangerous crossings.

The Ultimate and Most Important Survival Rule for Americans in Britain

The rule is: Look both ways every time you want to cross a street. If this rule is not followed, inevitably a time will come when the visitor will suddenly find ferocious traffic hurtling from an unexpected direction. Injury or death might thereby become the end result of what was supposed to have been a wonderful trip to Britain. The author remembers one occasion in London when survival was a matter of an inch or two after a quick turn of the head revealed a gigantic, red double-decker bus rapidly approaching.

Since Americans have been conditioned all of their lives to look only in one direction for traffic, a habit has to be instilled to look *both* ways in Britain every time one crosses the street. In Britain, visitors will be surprised time and again by vehicles suddenly appearing where they did not expect them because the traffic moves on the left-hand side of the road. In London, there are actually signs printed in the pavement of the busiest streets to make Americans and Continental Europeans look to the right for traffic.

British children receive vigorous basic pedestrian survival training in their earliest years. It is equally important for Americans who bring their children to Britain to drill them on pedestrian safety.

Driving in Britain

Why Drive?

First of all, why drive at all? Buses and trains go almost everywhere, and long walks promote health. Taxis are abundant when a short car ride is unavoidable. Long before great masses of Britons began to buy their own cars, an extensive grid of relatively low-cost public rail and bus transportation had been laid out. Much like the inhabitant of Manhattan, the visitor simply does not need a car to enjoy Britain.

Most Americans are wedded to their cars and find

it difficult to spend time without having their own wheels available. America is a nation on wheels, particularly in places like Los Angeles or Cheyenne or Reno, where it is impossible to get around without one. For those who cannot break the habit of driving while in Britain, car rentals are readily available. A passport and a valid driver's license from one of the states are the only things required. Insurance is figured into the rental costs.

Renting a car is easy, but driving it around is not. Carefully consider the special circumstances of driving in Britain before investing a substantial part of your time behind a steering wheel.

Some Hazards of Driving in Britain: Heavy Traffic

In a way, driving in Britain is an attempt to carry on life as it is found at home. Much time, money, frustration and anxiety will be the overall price paid for having a car to drive in Britain, but there are those individuals who feel absolutely deprived, and, in the most extreme cases, emasculated, if they must do without command of their own wheels for any period of time.

At least half of the British of driving age still do not drive, although having or not having a car has come to be something of a clear status symbol. Even with millions not driving, Britain is so small that nearly all of the roads are terribly crowded. Outside of the major motorways, Britains's roads are for the most part old, narrow and inadequate to handle the streams of traffic that sail along most of them. The most daunting statistic about British traffic is simply this: Nowhere in the world are there more cars per mile of paved surface. Think about that before popping into a Hertz or Avis in Britain.

Some Hazards of Driving on the Opposite Side of the Road

The first thing to remember is never to refer to driving on the opposite side of the road as driving on the "wrong" side. Even if nearly all of the countries in the world keep to the right, the British and a few ex-colonies continue to drive on the left, and for them at least, it is definitely not the "wrong" side.

The second and more important thing to remember is that it is not as difficult as it seems during the first few horrifying moments. Most experienced drivers can adjust to it fairly easily.

The third and even more important thing to remember is that the steering wheel is always on the side where the white line is or ought to be. In America, it is on the left of the car and in Britain on the right. Of course, the white line in Britain is called the "divider."

Turns are difficult until the American driver realizes he or she must negotiate them just the opposite from the way that they are negotiated at home. Their left-hand turns are short and sharp, just as our right-hand turns are. For a right-hand turn in Britain, the driver must go out and over, just as Americans do for a left-hand turn. The key calculation is always to keep the "divider" on the side where the driver is.

One set of markings on paved roads is very helpful for making what at first appear to be strange turns. A broken line across one lane of an intersecting road means that lane is to be driven into. The solid line across the other lane indicates that it is not to be driven into.

On the big motorways, what Americans call interstate highways, the slower traffic will be on the left, and faster traffic will be expected to pass on the right.

The lane furthest to the right is the fastest lane, which is just the opposite of the arrangement in the United States. Americans tend to be sloppy about moving to a slower lane when someone comes up from behind at a faster speed. Most British drivers in a hurry will encourage a move to a slower lane by flashing lights, blaring horns and imposing, frightening tailgating.

For many people, the most difficult feat of driving on the opposite side involves judging distances on the left-hand side of the car when the steering wheel is over on the right. Experienced American drivers more or less automatically calculate distances on the passenger's side when it is on the right. Some people discover that switching to calculations of distances on the left can lead to curb scraping or worse. It takes time for such calculations to become more or less automatic.

Some Hazards of Driving in Britain: Roads, Roundabouts and Learners

British roads range from the sublime to the ridiculous. The best of them are similar to our interstate highways or freeways, except that, as mentioned before, faster cars pass on the right rather than on the left. These roads are called motorways, and have the designation "M" applied to them, with a number — M-1, M-2, etc. If they are divided highways having two or more lanes in either direction and some space between directions, they receive the odd sounding name of "dual carriageway." These roads allow 70 m.p.h. traffic, which is indicated by a circular sign with a black slash running through it diagonally.

Some Britons are proud of the engineering complexity of the intersections of their modern roads. One such complex of intersections, near Birmingham, has gained the popular name of "Spaghetti Junction." Those who marvel at all of the roads and ramps coming and going at this place ought to be invited for a day of freeway fun around Los Angeles!

The first class motorways of Britain were pushed through a densely populated and cluttered countryside on straight lines. Some of them followed the straight old Roman roads, marvels of engineering for their day. The rest of the roads in Britain tend to be tortuous, consisting of a never-ending series of curves, turns, dips, angles and bends. Moreover, towns, cars, trucks, people and the unexpected road hazard slow up every road. Ordinarily, a twenty-mile drive is an easy ride of twenty minutes in a western state; in Britain, a twenty-mile drive along a secondary road can be an ordeal of well over an hour.

The worst British roads are the very minor ones. Some are almost incredible, such as the one-lane tracts that have dense bushes and trees growing up on both sides. On some roads, the foliage meets overhead so that driving is like going down a long, twisting green tube. Suddenly, out of nowhere, an oncoming car can appear, and both cars will have to scratch into the vegetation so that they can pass each other.

At least these crooked and slow minor roads are free from a hazard that all of the major roads possess: roundabouts. These exist to handle traffic at junctions, usually where more than two roads intersect. On American interstates, an elaborate set of cloverleafs, ramps, overpasses and underpasses handles such situations, but Britain does not have the space nor the resources for such arrangements. Instead, the roundabout takes traffic into a circle, which gives it its name. Roads shoot off the outer rim of the circle the way the spokes run off a wheel.

Roundabouts can be maddening. Traffic is supposed to slow at one of these vehicular merry-go-rounds, and it does somewhat, but not enough to take the pressure off the driver careening around with a stream of traffic roaring right behind. Cars will cut in front to make fast and dramatic exits. The driver has to make an exit somewhere also, and hopes that it will be undramatic. If you miss your exit on a roundabout, go all the way around the circle again and try once more. All the while, it is necessary to strain to see the road signs so that the proper exit can be taken.

Drivers who are just learning can be more dangerous on roundabouts than in other situations. Learners are everywhere in Britain, readily identifiable by the big letter "L" that they are required to post on their cars. They should be given leeway and consideration. Perhaps rental agencies should offer "LA" signs for "Learning Americans"!

How Most British Drivers Drive

Overall, the British are good drivers. They have to be in order to keep their vehicles out of the junk shop. Americans driving in Britain can count on most of the people on the road being quick, alert and precise.

Down any major British road, cars travel almost bumper to bumper, in a steady, maddening roar of traffic. Even the most polite British drivers tailgate in a manner that would be exceptional in any state, including New York and California. The American driver in Britain who continues to follow his rule of thumb to leave one car length of space per each ten miles per hour of speed will soon find that someone will zip in between him or her and the car ahead.

One curious custom of British drivers is to give a

quick flash of the headlights. This is not an official legal signal, but custom has made it standard practice on British roads. A quick flash of the headlights in daytime or of the high beam at night means, "I see you" or "I know what you are up to" or "Go ahead. I am watching out for you." This very civilized practice is most helpful on Britain's difficult roads. Perhaps it could be followed to advantage in the United States as well.

Much of this flashing goes on when cars opt to pass. Passing in Britain can be a breathtaking experience. All two-lane roads magically become three-lane roads in the minds of British drivers who make their move to pass. The British driver does not always wait until there are no oncoming cars, as any sensible driver would do in the United States. British drivers just go ahead and pass, feeling secure in the assumption that the oncoming driver will see him or her, flash, and then pull far over towards the side of the road so that the passing car, the passed car and the oncoming car can all be accommodated, if need be, three across at one split second of time. Driving in Britain affords many such thrilling moments.

Another characteristic of British drivers is that they seem to have a fear of wearing out their batteries. Therefore, they put on their lights as late in the day as possible. Some have said that the decision to flick them on does not occur until the driver cannot see five feet beyond his fenders. British drivers are likely to run for hours in the darkening gloom on just their parking lights, sometimes creating the specter of a swarm of fireflies zooming down a busy road.

Keen observers have pointed out that the British class system imposes itself on motoring also. Rolls Royces and their ilk do seem to push Morris Minors and Ford Fiestas out of the way with sublime arrogance. Big expensive cars and small cheap cars do not appear to have the same right of way in Britain. Perhaps a sociologist or psychologist will take up this subject.

Another Hazard: Gas Prices

When the pound is strong, gas prices in Britain are likely to be twice as high as prices in the United States. This might seem odd, considering that Britain pumps so much petroleum from the North Sea that it can export the substance. Nevertheless, Britain has had a long tradition of high taxes on gasoline, which is called petrol. At least the British gallon, or imperial gallon, is larger.

Another consoling thought is that Britain is a small country. One brutally hard day of driving on American interstate highways would take a car from the northernmost tip of Scotland to the farthest southeastern tip of England, the greatest distance that could be driven in one direction in Britain. Most people, most of the time, drive distances that would be considered short by nearly all Americans, except, perhaps, those on the eastern coastal plain.

The Vocabulary of the Car

The following terms with their translations might be helpful for the American who finds him- or herself stranded in a British garage somewhere:

These words will be helpful on the roads of Britain:

An *articulated lorry* is the word for a tractor trailer truck.

A *caravan* is the British word for a trailer, or any addition that functions as a recreational vehicle.

A *car park* is the British word for parking lot, and serves as another example of the directness of British English.

A *divider* is the line or strip in the middle of the road dividing traffic.

Dual carriageway is the British term for a divided highway.

An *estate car* is the British term for a station wagon.

A *gallon* in Britain is larger than a gallon in America. Britain's imperial gallon holds 277.42 cubic inches of liquid; the American gallon holds 231 cubic inches.

A *junction* in Britain means the same thing as it does in America but it is applied differently. Curiously, Americans usually use the word for railroads and say "intersection" when they mean a coming together of roads. British people refer to a junction of roads.

A *lorry* is truck.

M.O.T. is the abbreviation for Ministry of Transport. Applied to cars, especially in classified sales ads, M.O.T. means that the car has passed the ministry's rather stringent inspection requirements. A M.O.T. sticker on the windshield permits the vehicle to operate.

Nearside is the British word for the part of the road that is near the sidewalk.

Number plate is the British word for license plate.

Offside is the British word for the side away from the sidewalk.

Petrol in Britain means gasoline.

Verge is the British word for a strip of grass on the edge of a highway, what Americans would call a shoulder, although ours are apt to be paved rather than grassy.

Trains

After considering all of the hazards and difficulties of driving in Britain, giving up the use of cars would seem to be a very sensible thing to do, particularly if the amount of time available is short. Fast trains go to most of the more significant places several times a day.

Except for Amtrak, long-distance travel by train is passé in the United States. It still flourishes in Britain, although competition from road traffic has sapped much of its revenue, made some of its lines obsolete and led to the shrinking of the railway grid. Britain was the pioneering nation for rail travel, just as the United States has pioneered in the air. Therefore, Britons still have a soft spot for train travel because all of the excitement and glamour and romance that Americans associate with plane travel was once expressed for train travel in Britain. The speed, power and magnitude of railways simply dazzled Victorian Britons.

The basic fact that Britain is a small country has the greatest advantage for train travel. The rail grid is still elaborate, despite recent shrinkage. Service to important destinations is frequent, and trains generally run on time. It takes only a glance at a Britrail map to show that trains still go almost everywhere. Incidentally, child visitation problems for divorced and mobile British parents are lessened because it is possible to travel almost everywhere to all of Britain in less than a day.

Trains vary enormously in appearance and performance. Less-traveled routes have small, rumbling trains that are more like trolleys. The main routes are connected by the powerful "Intercity" diesel trains, which Americans would call super express trains. The Intercity trains are painted yellow at both ends, and when they approach their reputed 125 m.p.h., they literally live up to the their popular name of "flying banana." In between the streamlined Intercity trains and the quaint trolley-like trains are a number of intermediate trains, some fast and some slow, some with rather sparse interiors and some with upholstered compartments that seem right out of old film sets.

Train travel has great advantages for Americans in Britain. First, all of the hassles and confusions of the motorways can be avoided, as well as the need to find a parking place. Second, trains can provide a good way to observe and meet ordinary British people. All kinds of people can be found on the trains, ranging from brightly outfitted football (soccer) fans to staid businessmen complete with *The Times*, briefcase, conservative suit and umbrella. Frequently, British travelers will politely, subtly and silently observe the American observer. Conversations will have to be initiated by the visitor in most cases. Most Britons will be quite willing to talk to visitors at length, but they will not hail a visitor breezily in the American manner.

Buses in Britain

The best that can be said about British buses is that they are cheap, often costing less than half of rail fares to the same destination. The worst that can be said is that they may turn out to be roaring rattletraps. Americans should not expect ordinary British buses to have the comforts of large interstate buses at home. In fact, most do not even have toilets. If the visitor is lucky and gets aboard a shiny, new vehicle, the journey ahead must nevertheless negotiate all of the hazards I have already indicated.

Long distance journeys on British buses can be tiring on a crowded vehicle, particularly for non-smokers who are too close to the fumes of the smoking section. The infrequent rest stops can bring the traveler to the grimmest and dingiest of British cafés. Even so, buses do go almost everywhere at low cost, and so provide another opportunity to observe ordinary, workaday Britain.

In London, the location to board long distance buses is the Victoria Coach Station, which is only one block from the Victoria Railway Station. The Green Line Coaches can be picked up in various locations that are designated by green signs. These buses operate between London and its surrounding area.

Getting Around in London: The Underground

Having your own car or driving a rented car in central London is very difficult and, as I have indicated, the individual is better off without one.

For the relatively affluent, capacious London cabs abound. Their drivers are good, generally honest, and all must pass rigorous tests on the geography of London's streets before they are licensed to ply their trade.

Most people, however, will do most of their travel on the underground, otherwise known as the "tube." It is London's remarkable subway system which provides abundant and rapid public transportation all over the London area. Buses roar everywhere over the surface of the metropolis, of course, but their routes, numbers, criss-crossing and diverging can become very confusing for the visitor. It is much better to depend on the "tube" because it is usually faster and more direct than any surface transportation.

In addition to being convenient, the underground is very interesting historically and sociologically. Most trains and stations are old, evoking memories of World War II, when people took shelter from Nazi bombs in the system's caverns. All sorts of interesting people can be observed on the tube, but the conventions respecting privacy in crowded places require that such observations be made discreetly. Conversations rarely occur, and when they do they are kept at low levels by most British people.

The underground radiates far out from the center of London in all directions, making it possible for many outlying square miles of greater London to be within a half hour or 45 minutes of Oxford Street or Piccadilly Circus or Charing Cross Station. Farther out than the most distant tube stations is a commuter rail network that feeds into the underground system. All of this enables literally millions of people to work in the metropolis without having to spend an excessive amount of time commuting.

Practical Hints for Using the Underground

At first the system seems difficult, but with some practice the visitor soon becomes delighted with his or her ability to zoom all over London. It can become great fun, especially when the person has a pre-purchased pass for unlimited rides.

The first step is to get a little folding map of the underground, which is available at all the stations. When first studied, the routes look much more complicated than they actually are. Notice the different colors for the different lines. Notice also the stations that appear as little solid notches. Observe that some stations are designated by round circles and others are designated by half circles that merge into other half circles. If a station has a circle or a merged circle, lines can be changed at them. This cannot be done at stations indicated by notches. At stations where changes can be made, signs prominently direct passengers to the other lines.

When you are riding on the tube, look at the chart of stations on the wall of the car above the windows. You can tick off the stations one by one on this chart because it gives only the line upon which you are riding. You can easily coordinate this chart with the little folding map.

Here are some other things to notice about the map. The Circle Line makes a complete circle. Observe, also, that some lines branch. For example, at the upper center of the map, the Northern Line will have one line going to Edgeware, another to Mill Hill East and another to High Barnet. If you are heading towards the center of London, these outward-bound destinations do not make any difference, but if you are heading north, it will be important to make sure that you get on the right branch. A heavy train arrival sign, which changes its notices electronically, will be hanging over the platform at stations of branching lines to tell you which train is coming next and which train is coming after that.

Fares can be paid in three different ways. First, you can buy your ticket at the booth in the station. Just say what your destination is. Second, if you have the exact change, you might want to eliminate standing in line at the booth by using one of the machines issuing tickets. Be sure to spot your destination on the list over the appropriate machine. At busy stations, tickets are validated by another machine. Simply watch how other people stick their tickets in the machines in order to open the turnstiles. The third way is to purchase a pass that enables you to travel anywhere on London's underground or on London's buses or on both systems. Such passes can be purchased for you in the United States by a travel agent at no extra charge. Such passes have various names: "Go as You Please," "Central Tube Rovers" and "Red Bus Rovers." The ones offering travel on bus and tube for a specific period of time can be real money savers and are highly recommended.

One more hint: Americans and other visitors have a penchant for idly standing all over the escalators. Signs clearly insist that they stand over to one side so that people may hurry up or down them. Even in polite London, hapless tourists can be barked aside, shoved aside or run over if they stand on the wrong side.

FOOD

Some Generalizations

Ordinary British food tends to be like British weather. It is mostly unexciting but there are a few bright spots amid the general dreariness. Unlike Germany or France, Britain does not have a celebrated cuisine redolent with special sauces and delectable combinations. At best, British food is similar to good American food. At worst, it is greasy and overcooked. At least it is better, on average, than Irish or Russian food, which does not really say all that much for it.

The British cook a few things quite well: simple, plain, unspiced roasts, particularly roast beef, for instance, or various kinds of fresh fish, also prepared simply. Pubs often serve good British food inexpensively at midday. From this "pub grub," as it is called, "shepherd's pie" can be recommended. It is a simple concoction of ground meat and onions covered with mashed potatoes.

British food has its chamber of horrors also. One of the most reliable ways to encounter bad British food is to go to a cheap short order restaurant. Many of them are called cafés, and they all tend to bask in the glare of fluorescent light and have a deafening level of noise from the roar of the cooking grease, the semi-intelligible shouts of the staff and the endless clatter of heavy dishes. Here one can sample the family of meat pies. The British love to bake pies around concoctions of meat. Pork pies deserve their notoriety. They have the specific gravity of lead, and they can be thrown just like hand grenades or baseballs. One can remove the pie crust and expect to find a layer of shiny green gelatinous scum. Inside this layer is a core of pinkish, grayish pork that looks as if it is composed of ground snouts or tails. Steak and kidney pies are another British culinary wonder. British people always insist that it is very fine when it is cooked just right, but they forever complain that their particular steak and kidney pie is overdone or, something worse, underdone, when the kidneys do, alas, remind one of their essential function when they were embedded in a living animal. Yorkshire pudding, although widely celebrated, seems to be only pastry made in the grease that comes from roasting.

None of these British pie dishes do much for the calorie or blood cholesterol count, but concern for a healthier diet does not manifest itself among British people to the extent that it does among Americans. This can be said for poorer Britons especially. They are not likely to encounter health foods and low fat products. This typically American dietary phenomenon will in all likelihood come into wider use in Britain in the future. American fast foods certainly have. The golden arches of McDonald's can be seen all over, although the food at such places tends to be more expensive and its arrival slower than in the United States.

Britain's old, original fast food was "Fish and Chips." Nowadays, there are several kinds of fast food fish and chips establishments in Britain as well as in the United States, all gleaming in aluminum and plastic under the ever present fluorescent lights. These new places do not serve the traditional proletarian fish and chips, which consisted of a hunk of unspecified fish in a puff of fried batter accompanied by a mass of greasy fried potatoes. All of this used to be served up in a cone of ordinary newspaper that rapidly became translucent with grease. Rough looking characters used to be seen propped up in doorways clawing into their greasy cones for this old staple of the British diet. Today, with fish much more expensive, the cheap hamburger seems to have become something of a replacement. The chips, by the way, are what we call french fried potatoes. The British word for what we call potato chips is "crisps." These are essential vocabulary words for all young Americans in Britain.

In Britain, vegetables can suffer a fate as horrible as that of the coagulated meat pie. "Veg" usually means peas, but on poorer menus brussels sprouts can be substituted. Peas can plop onto plates cooked to death, all concave and grayish green. Brussels sprouts can be so overcooked that a simple thrust with a fork can cause them to explode like a green caterpillar under foot.

British Imperial Food: The Best Bargain in Britain

A clear indication of Britain's imperial past can be found in its food. London and all of the major towns and cities have numerous Indian and Chinese restaurants which offer tasty and cheap meals.

Since Americans are ordinarily well acquainted with Chinese food, there is no point in describing it here. But the location of London's Chinatown is worth pointing out because there are so many restaurants of such a great variety crammed into one particular section. London's Chinatown is just behind Trafalgar Square, a few blocks to the northwest along Gerrard and Lisle streets. Seafood specialties, Peking style and Szechwan style, can be readily obtained. Britain has had a long connection with China through extensive trading activity and the acquisition of Hong Kong. Chinese people also migrated to British Malaya and Singapore and took jobs in the worldwide British maritime navy. No wonder that substantial numbers of Chinese came to Britain, bringing their wonderful ways of cooking with them.

The cuisine of the Indian subcontinent is a special glory in Britain, and something that most Americans are unfamiliar with. It is rather unfair to call the cuisine simply "Indian" because Bangladesh and Pakistan have contributed their share of people and restaurants to the British scene. Nevertheless, when the British were in India it was all together in one political entity. On that basis, the name Indian will be used to refer to the restaurants of Pakistan and Bangladesh as well.

Anglo-Indian relations have a long history. The British were active in India as traders and administrators long before the American Revolution. In India, British influence can still be seen everywhere, and in Britain, Indian influence can be found in art and architecture, but above all, in the presence of people from the Indian subcontinent. They and their aromatic restaurants are ubiquitous.

Neither Indians nor their restaurants can be found in many parts of the United States, particularly in the American West. As a result, many Americans in Britain hesitate to patronize Indian restaurants in Britain. Some shy away because they are reluctant to try something new, and others have negative images of a starving, dirty, impoverished Indian subcontinent. The fact that the economic and social problems of the Indian subcontinent mean high death rates, terrible slums and massive malnutrition does not necessarily preclude the existence of wealthy, healthy and prosperous groups in the same region, and these people are very well nourished on very delicately and richly spiced foods.

American visitors should not be daunted by the exotic aromas and sights of good Indian food, nor should they be afraid of being seared by hot dishes because Indian fare ranges from mild to medium to hot to very hot. Waiters are very helpful to newcomers pondering what might seem to be a strange menu, and they are usually very willing to make recommendations to help customers steer away from the hot dishes. Sometimes language problems intrude when an American accent and an Indian accent mutually lower the level of intelligibility.

Americans from the Southwest who regularly enjoy hot Mexican food should not become overconfident in an Indian restaurant. The very hot dishes, such as Vindaloo curry and Madras meat, can numb mouth and tongue totally and put the sinus system out of commission for a day or more. These dishes come from the hottest regions of India. Visitors should always try dishes from the cooler, mountain regions and the milder, wetter regions along the coasts of the Indian Ocean because they are mild, featuring gentle, bland spices.

Besides offering a great variety of curries for meat and vegetables, Indian cuisine features rice dishes, many of them called Biriani, various appetizers and carefully roasted items, many of which are in the Tandoori fashion. For some people, Indian food seems to be addictive. In the most extreme cases, a real craving for curry can occur. British people have no problems with such addictions because there will always be an Indian restaurant somewhere down the next street or so, but for Americans who become addicted, curry withdrawal pangs can afflict them when they return to the United States. Mexican food can help somewhat in overcoming this condition. The danger of withdrawal symptoms notwithstanding, no American visitor to Britain should bypass the opportunity of trying Indian food.

The British Vocabulary for Food and Drink

Of course, there is no comparison between the effort required to decipher a menu in a French restaurant and that expended with a British one. Most of the words found on British and American menus are identical, but there are some terms that need to be translated or explained.

Food

An *aubergine* is an eggplant.

A *banger* is a particular kind of bland sausage.

A *biscuit* is a British word for a cookie or a cracker.

A *cornet* is their word for cone, such as an ice cream cone.

Clotted cream is super thick cream, a specialty of Devon and Cornwall, places that probably produce the richest and thickest ice cream in all the world.

Cold usually does not mean ice cold, as it does in America. This condition in Britain is often what Americans would call cool.

Corn is a word for all grains. The American word corn is translated as maize or Indian corn. It grows poorly in Britain and is usually an animal food in those parts of Europe where it does grow.

Chips are french fried potatoes in Britain.

Courgettes are zucchini.

Crisps are potato chips. Note the British translation of chips just above.

Flan is a pie that has no top on it.

Gateau is a rich, fancy cake, but the term has come to be applied to cakes in general.

Greens are green vegetables, usually peas.

Ice can mean ice or ice cream.

A *joint* is a piece of meat for roasting.

Minced meat or *mince* is what Americans call chopped beef or hamburger meat.

Mixed grill is a main dish consisting of several diverse kinds of grilled meat with some vegetables too.

Plaice is a flat European fish that resembles and tastes like flounder.

Scotch egg is a hard-boiled egg embedded in a brownish pastry crust.

Shepherd's pie is ground meat and onions covered with mashed potatoes. It is usually quite good.

Starters are the items Americans would call appetizers or the first course.

Sweet can mean either a dessert or a piece of candy. The plural form, sweets, means candy.

Treacle is a very sweet liquid, like molasses, to be poured over a dessert.

Tin means a can, so tinned is the British word for canned.

Underdone means rare.

Drink

Bitter is the most widely consumed beer. It is literally more bitter than American beer, being darker and heavier.

Cuppa is slang for a cup of tea and is a very colloquial expression. Cups of tea are downed at regular intervals by British people during the workday and before and after it.

Jar is slang for a pint of beer.

Lager is like light ale in America.

Pale ale is light in color and body.

Pint means a pint of beer, filling a glass that is just a little larger than an American pint.

Shandy is a light drink of beer mixed with lemonade or ginger beer. It is the drink that genteel ladies used to be expected to sip.

Stout is a heavy, dark, sweet beer. The most devastating variety is imported by tanker from Ireland and looks like heavy motor oil capped by foam.

Whiskey means scotch.

TELEVISION AND RADIO

Watching television and listening to the radio are such time-consuming preoccupations in America that the visitor to Britain is likely to sample British fare and make comparisons with electronic entertainment at home.

One surprise that Americans encounter is that there are comparatively few channels. Another surprise is that so many American programs are run, most of them of dubious quality. Probably the greatest surprise of all is the power and prevalence of public broadcasting. While Britain does have independent television and radio stations, complete with many, many commercials, the British Broadcasting Corporation, or the BBC, dominates the media. The "Beeb," as it is known colloquially, derives much of its income from taxes paid directly on television sets and radios in the form of licenses for their operation. Its governing board functions independently as a corporation, and every effort is made to insure that its membership is skilled, professional and nonpolitical. This structure, based upon an appreciation of the need to have a free and independent media, keeps the BBC from coming under the control of the Prime Minister and the Cabinet.

There are other advantages of the BBC that are enjoyed directly by the viewer. The standards of quality are high, since from the beginning of its existence the BBC has been charged with elevating and educating the whole British public. Critics can point out that this often leads to programming that is overly serious and pretentious, to the extent that comic satire has had a field day imitating it. In fact, there are Americans who see BBC for the first time and think that they are watching a comic skit.

The BBC actually runs several channels at once, which allows lighter entertainment and regional specialties to appear. The blessing of all BBC offerings is that they are free from commercials and the pressures that sponsors might impose.

Public broadcasting in the United States is crippled by being underfinanced. Some of its best programs are actually from the comparatively well-financed BBC. For the careful observer, TV watching in Britain can be a remarkably rewarding experience. Proponents of increased support for public broadcasting in the United States will find much to confirm their view in Britain.

The same can be said for radio. It is never difficult to pull in classical music, jazz, comedies or mysteries on the radio, particularly on the BBC stations. There is also an amazing array of freewheeling private radio. Americans are surprised at how enduringly some of the hits of yesterday continue on the airwaves in Britain today.

A FEW PRACTICAL HINTS ON LUGGAGE

A most important point to make about luggage is that nearly everyone takes too much of it to Britain. Americans bring too many clothes, too many gadgets and too much varied stuff. Hauling unnecessary bulk around becomes a drag very quickly. This admonition has been made time and time again, but it is one of the most difficult to get anyone to adhere to.

Another helpful hint is to be a loose packer, a person who leaves extra space in suitcases. This, that and the other thing picked up along the way will take up the extra space very quickly.

Do not take clothes in the fond expectation of spending time among the British people who dress for the famous horseraces, regattas and official cermonies. The tiniest percentage of the population ever dresses like that, and Americans going to Britain cannot expect to join the Queen's set.

Some American students planning a trip to Britain will be relieved to know that British students frequently dress in attire that can be called super ratty. Old, worn, drab, ill-matched and even ragged clothes can be seen wherever British students abound.

Everyone should remember that Britain is a very civilized country where friendly shopkeepers in well-stocked shops all speak English. What this means is that you can buy anything you need easily, and if you are debating how much underwear or how many sweaters to bring, decide to take the minimal number. If you are short of any items in Britain, buy them there.

Many Americans come from parts of the United States that have much less rain than Britain. They should give special attention to bringing what will keep them dry, particularly their heads and feet. Umbrellas really are needed in Britain any time of the year.

CHAPTER TWO

Understanding British Geography and Economics

THE PARTS THAT MAKE UP BRITAIN

National Designations: When to Say British Rather Than English, Welsh or Scottish

Americans often have problems with national designations in Britain. The official name of the country is the United Kingdom, abbreviated as U.K. Before World War II, "Great Britain" was the usual designation. Today, "Britain" is still used, usually without "Great." All of these names refer to the whole of the largest island in that archipelago, or cluster of islands, known to geographers as the "British Isles." Of the remaining islands, only Ireland is of substantial size.

Most of Ireland is, of course, a sovereign republic that is separate from the U.K. The rest of the islands are quite small, such as the Scilly Islands in the English Channel and the Shetlands and Orkneys, which are sprinkled in the cold waters north of Britain.

All the people on the island of Britain can safely be called "British." This includes the English, the Welsh and the Scots, the three nationalities that are constitutionally united and comprise the "United Kingdom." Of the three nationalities, the English predominate overwhelmingly in numbers and take up most of the space on Britain.

Most of the English were originally descendants of the taller and blonder Anglo-Saxons, the Germanic people who once drove the shorter and darker-haired Celtic people and other early types into the hills of the north and the west. Of course, the mixing, mingling and moving of people over the centuries have made the English population quite a hodgepodge.

The predominance of the English on Britain, along with their language, customs, laws and history, has been so strong that foreigners often make the serious mistake of calling non-English British persons "English." For a Welsh or Scottish person, this is as infuriating as calling a Coloradan a Texan or someone from Philadelphia, a New Yorker. The Welsh are British, but not English; the Scots are British, but not English; the English are both English and British. Visitors should be very careful about this point. When in doubt, British is always a safe term.

The Parts of Britain: England's Regions

The largest component of Britain, England, can itself be divided into several regions (see map). East

The Parts of the Island of Britain

Anglia is a remarkably flat area bulging out on the eastern part of the island. It is similar in topography to the Netherlands, which is directly across the North Sea. The "Midlands" are in the middle of the rolling, undulating plains of England, and include the lands that are the farthest from the sea in all of Britain, which never exceeds a grand total of only 70 miles! There is a great conurbation in the west Midlands, centering around Birmingham. Very picturesque places are to be found in the Cotswold region just east of the Bristol Channel. The "West Country" is the region that juts out into the Atlantic along the southern tail of Britain. Since it has rough country, moors and charming little seaport towns, it is deservedly popular with tourists. Devon and Cornwall are the shires of the West Country. The "south" is a term sometimes used to describe the counties south of the Thames, a region with a reputation for affluence, culture and, alas, snobbery. The "north," an area actually north of the Midlands, contrasts sharply with the "south." It has many sections developed in recent centuries that are rougher and obviously more industrial than in the south. Even so, the people living in the north seem less reserved and much more informal than in the south of England. Two important counties in the north are worth noting: Lancashire and Yorkshire. The former is associated with the very first developments of the industrial revolution. Yorkshire is huge compared to other counties, and is something of the Texas of England. The westernmost part of Yorkshire is grim and industrial, but the other sections, which are called "ridings," have some ruggedly beautiful stretches of green hillsides and foggy moors.

The Parts of Britain: Wales and the Welsh

Wales is not very large and not heavily populated. England is over six times as large as Wales and has almost 47 million people. Wales has only 2.8 million persons. Nevertheless, England and most of the English-speaking parts of the world have had a substantial Welsh addition to their populations. The Welsh who have remained in their homeland are spread across a poor but lovely land. Blue hills, dark mountains, gemlike small towns and golden beaches are found throughout north and central Wales. In south Wales, a depressed conurbation runs along the southern coast of the region. Cardiff, the capital of Wales, and several other cities are located along this strip, which is dependent upon coal mining and industry.

The Welsh are extremely proud of their history, a subject not unmixed with legend. They see themselves as the original and true Britons, the people who fought with the Romans long before Anglo-Saxons arrived. When the Anglo-Saxons invaded, the outnumbered Britons fought them also, until they were pushed into the hills of the west, which became Wales. There they remained, a fierce, pastoral, tribal hill people until English kings sent expeditions to subdue them. The great castles of Wales testify to the force that England brought to bear to conquer and subdue Wales. Militant contemporary Welsh nationalists claim that the conquest was never complete, right down to the present day. Some of them deface English names on roadsigns and agitate for Welsh language programming on radio and television. Actually, only a small percentage of the Welsh population regularly speaks the Welsh language today.

A vivid stereotype of the Welsh exists. It has them

as great singers and talkers of quick wit, with a romantic streak and a tendency to be somewhat sly and shifty. It also depicts them as short, dark-haired and dark-eyed. They are seen at their very best when singing hymns in their plain Protestant chapels. The stereotype makes much of their Celtic nature, which links them to the Scots, the Irish and the Bretons of Brittany in France. Yet they differ from these other Celts, but not from the Scots, in being staunch Protestants.

Among the famous Welshmen of history have been Henry VII, the founder of the Tudor dynasty; David Lloyd George, the Prime Minister during World War I; and Richard Burton, the actor.

The Parts of Britain: Scotland and the Scots

Behind many stereotypes lie some truths. This certainly seems to be the case for the proverbial Scottish thriftiness. The Scots do not seem to waste anything, and they do make very careful and open efforts to find out about prices and values. A stark geographical reality has made thriftiness a necessity over the centuries. Scotland has been a very poor country during all the centuries when agriculture dominated the economy. The soil is hard with rocks and flint in most places, and the growing season is short. Most of the rugged and beautiful stretches of Highland Scotland simply cannot produce much food. For centuries, Scots have huddled in their chilly, rain-drenched cottages or slate gray buildings eating oatmeal. Big spenders do not come from such raw environments.

The most prosperous part of Scotland has always been the Lowland zone, stretching from the North Sea in the east to the Irish Sea in the west, just above the rough border country separating England from Scotland. It has the best farming conditions in Scotland. The population is mixed with Anglo-Saxons in this zone, while Celts predominate in the Highland region to the north. Edinburgh (pronounced *Ed-in-boro*), the captivating romantic, ancient capital, lies in the eastern part of this zone, along an indentation of the ocean called the Firth of Forth. Edinburgh is filled with historic sights, especially along the Royal Mile running from Holyrood Palace to Edinburgh Castle (see the section on Using Limited Time Effectively in Britain). At the western end of the Lowland zone is the second most famous Scottish city, Glasgow (pronounced *Glas-go,* not *Glas-gow*), unfortunately noted today for extremely high rates of unemployment and considerable crime, as well as for industries that are old, tired and depressed. There are also several other significant urban areas in the Lowland zone.

Highland Scotland has Britain's ruggedest mountains, and best hunting, fishing and skiing regions. Such well-developed recreational opportunities make the Highlands a popular place for vacationers. While visiting Americans might enjoy the scenery and the small towns of this region, they should always recognize that the United States has vast recreational resources along these lines. Americans are better off spending their time in Britain at places that cannot be duplicated or surpassed at home.

A sprinkle of fairly new looking towns thinly covers the Highland zone. In the past, fierce tribal clans occupied Highland Scotland, warring upon each other and, when opportunities arose, raiding either the Lowland region or the north of England. Hardy Highlanders maintained their traditions of bagpiping, wearing tartans and kilts, and dancing in a peculiarly Scottish manner long after the Lowland Scots had become anglicized.

For a time in the eighteenth century, just after the English brutally put down the last Scottish risings, these Scottish accouterments were banned, but they survived nonetheless. Yet today it can be difficult to see a kilt or hear a bagpipe in many parts of Scotland during the winter. This clannish paraphernalia from the Highlands really comes out in full force only during tourist season.

Scotland's topography has some distinct features in addition to the existence of these two zones. Long indentations of the coastline carry ocean water far towards the interior. These "firths" are similar to the "fjords" of Norway. The Firth of Forth, for instance, brings a long sweep of the ocean in just north of Edinburgh. In western and northern Scotland, a highly irregular coastline produces a vast number of islands and peninsulas.

Scotland has a nationalism that has been described as much more deeply rooted than that of the Welsh. When the Welsh were conquered, they were without their own Parliament, national church and national legal system. Scotland had all of these institutions, and technically Scotland was never conquered. England and Scotland were joined together in 1603 when a Scottish king, James VI, also became the king of England as James I. James VI and I, as he is often known, was the closest heir to Queen Elizabeth I, who died unmarried.

Before James, Scotland had been a very independent kingdom, often involved in alliances with France directed against England. On several occasions during Anglo-French wars, Scottish forces attacked through England's back door, the northern border. There were many brutal battles between the English and the Scots over the centuries, the last of which was the "Forty-five," an uprising of Highlanders in favor of the exiled Stuart pretender to the English throne. It occurred in 1745, just thirty years before the American Revolution began.

Scottish nationalism is understandable against this background of separate institutional development going far back into the Middle Ages, and it was reinforced by several wars against the English. Today Scottish nationalism is a potent force, although the majority of Scots probably realize their advantages in a United Kingdom. Certainly, the British government has tried to respect Scottish and Welsh sensitivities by accepting some forms of regional autonomy and by recognizing cultural differences. For example, it is not surprising to have a BBC announcer speaking with a distinctive Scots dialect. Another example is the use of Scottish pound notes issued by the Bank of Scotland. Scottish pounds have exactly the same worth as British pounds.

Like the Welsh, the Scots are all over the world. The English have joked that the British Empire was created so that the Scots could have a large area in which to make money. The Scots have retorted that if it were not for the famous regiments of Scots soldiers, such as the Black Watch, the British Empire could not have been created in the first place. The Scots have always seen their regiments as the best in the British army. Such banter reveals the ongoing rivalry between the English and the Scots, which is usually friendly and appreciative, but sometimes takes an edge.

The Scottish stereotype prevailing in America tends to be very favorable, depicting Scots as democratic, friendly and utterly thrifty. By the way, Americans do sometimes err in calling them "Scotch," which is the proper name for a beverage, but not for the Scots people.

The Scottish stereotype in England retains the thrifty aspect, sometimes stretching it into a mean stinginess. The English are apt to stress aspects of Celtic wildness in the Scots also. At their worst, the Scots are depicted as drinking to excess, and being tactless, blunt, crude, coarse and loud. Some unfriendly critics have suggested that these negative traits explain why the Scots have a reputation for getting on easier with Americans, since Americans at their worst are supposed to manifest these characteristics also. In Scotland, the worst stereotype of the Englishman can be just as unflattering. He is seen as effeminate, silly, insincere, devious, stiff, haughty, unfriendly and so cold-blooded that most human feelings have been drained out of him.

These stereotypes, friendly and unfriendly, along with those for the Irish and the Welsh, figure in that endless series of jokes that begin: "Once there was an Englishman, a Scotsman, a Welshman and an Irishman . . . ." American visitors are advised not to join this play upon national differences that have been created by geography and history over the centuries.

SIGNIFICANT ASPECTS OF BRITISH GEOGRAPHY

Size and Density

From an American standpoint, Britain is incredibly small and incredibly crowded. All of Britain is only 94,222 square miles, which means that all of it fits into the single state of Colorado (104,247 square miles) with 10,000 square miles left over. Perhaps Oregon would be more appropriate for the purposes of comparison, considering the cool and rainy climate encountered there. Britain can fit into Texas almost three times.

Britain's comparatively small land area was home to a grand total of 56,100,000 persons according to the census of 1980, almost a quarter of the total population of the United States. In 1980, Britain had 594 people per square mile, and the United States had 64. Our individual states vary greatly: Nevada has only 7.3 persons per square mile; Alaska, 0.7; Wyoming, 4.9; Colorado, 28; Texas, 54; California, 151; Connecticut, 637.8; and Rhode Island, 897.8. When Britain is divided into its component parts, England's density is shown to be formidable: 927 people per square mile. Wales, with so many beautiful mountains, has 345; and Scotland only has 168 people per square mile.

These stark figures show what visitors soon come to realize: thick throngs of people are everywhere in Britain. In most places, the masses of shoppers are dense; thoroughfares are crowded; strollers are found in thick knots in the countryside; every historic site or museum or cathedral has an ample audience every hour that it is open. American visitors will come to appreciate the space and solitude available to them in so many places at home.

While the density of population becomes readily apparent, the smallness of the country does not. There are so many regions, so many dialects, so many local styles and so much packed into so small a space that Britain really does seem like a much larger nation than it actually is. It feels as if Britain were once much larger, and had been shrunk in every direction some time long ago. This contention may not be as silly as it might seem at first. Given the limited mobility of people during all of the centuries before the railways, a single mile had to seem a greater distance than today. To a medieval peasant, going even twenty miles was probably an awesome journey. So all of those aspects that we variously label as provincialism, localism and regionalism were deeply rooted in Britain over very long periods of time. Their survivals, plus the compacted intermingling of urban and rural areas, give a sense of size that is illusory.

The Topography of Britain: A Man- or Woman-Sized Country

One old generalization about Britain's land surface is that it was designed to be man-sized or, as we would properly express it, woman-sized as well. What this means is that nature does not overwhelm. There are no awesome and seemingly impassable deserts or mountain ranges nor are there any torrential rivers or formidable swamps. The rain-fed rivers of Britain gently flow towards the sea; the mountains are old and worn, and the highest peaks only reach a few thousand feet. There are no deserts, and most of the marshy areas were drained long ago. While the weather often is depressing and miserable, blizzards or heat waves that kill droves of people do not occur as they do in America. So, in general, Britain is a gentle, green country providing a most agreeable environment for masses of Homo sapiens.

Whatever exceptional weather the British have is apt to be highly exaggerated, particularly in the more sensational press. For example, an ice storm that left a sheen of ice was once described as a "killer ice blizzard" because a motorist had skidded on it, hit a tree and died. When buses and trains occasionally have a problem with snow and ice, the situation produces headlines that scream: "Public Transportation Paralyzed!" All of these British journalists should be treated to a genuine storm whipping off the Rocky Mountains or a tornado in Kansas or Nebraska.

The Climate: The Influence of the Ocean

The effect of the Atlantic on Britain's climate is paramount. The ocean cools the island in summer and warms it in winter. Were it not for the warm flow of the Gulf Stream that brings water up from the south, Britain might have a climate similar to that of Labrador, which surprisingly occupies the same latitude as Britain.

Overall, due to the effect of the ocean, Britain's temperatures are moderate and predictable. High sixties can be expected in the summer and low forties in the winter, year after year. Stark extremes of weather, such as broiling weeks of 100° in summers and bitter below-zero weeks in winter are Continental phenomena found in such places far inland as the plains of Eurasia or the plains of the American Midwest.

The ocean plays an important role in shaping British attitudes and lifestyles. Insularity — the condition of being an island surrounded by the ocean — gives a feeling of separateness and independence. The old joke about the headline that read "Fog in the Channel — Continent Isolated!" reveals something essential about the British viewpoint. Moreover, the ocean has always been a grand playground for British people, whether they sail on it or swim in it, or frolic at an array of seaside resorts. Also, seafood has been a much more important part of the traditional British diet than in most parts of America.

British Weather: Mostly Agony with Some Ecstasy

The ocean also brings rain very, very regularly. Prevailing winds from the west lift clouds of moisture out of the Atlantic to drench Britain all year long. These clouds hang low and gray over the island day in and day out, with few exceptions. The most typical British weather forecast is for "sunny intervals," meaning that most of the day cloud and rain will prevail. Three-hundred days of precipitation per year can be expected in Britain, providing a stark contrast to the three-hundred days or more of sunshine that is the boast of some of the states in the sunbelt.

In the winter, visitors can expect Britain to be cold and wet. In the spring, it will still be cold and wet. In the summer, it becomes cool and wet, and occasionally warm and wet. In the fall, it becomes cold and wet again. Since dreary gray skies and raw rain are inevitable in Britain most of the year, many British people become masochistic over the weather and dwell endlessly on how they suffer from it.

Nevertheless, the climate does afford a few compensations. Britain is always bright green. Even after the rare occasional snowfall, visitors can push the snow aside and see bright green grass growing beneath. The Atlantic moisture keeps Britain lush with grass and other plants all year long. As one resident put it, Britain has a marvelous climate for plants, but a climate that is less agreeable for people and animals. In the south, roses can be seen blooming any month of year, and at least some dormant but hardy green vegetables can be harvested during the coldest months of winter.

Britain's general chilly mildness means that even in mid-winter, "frosts," or times when the temperature dips below 32°F, are specially reported on the radio or TV. Snow is exceptional, particularly in the south. When it does accumulate, it is expected to turn to slush and go away by itself. If it does not, it is usually pounded into an icy, gray crust on thoroughfares.

Overall mildness notwithstanding, the cold of Britain has a peculiarly penetrating effect that seems to chill to the very marrow of the bone. Extremely high humidity is probably responsible for this. British people cope with these damp chills by wearing layers of clothes, particularly thick sweaters.

While many American visitors have a difficult time with the damp chill, they usually have an easier time than the British in experiencing the occasional hot and humid days that show up in July and August. There are authenticated stories of British workers who threw down their tools and refused to work when the temperature went into the low eighties, protesting against the "inhuman conditions" of labor in such heat. Dallas construction workers staying at work during a 100°F heat wave provide an interesting contrast.

Even though it might not be appreciated, the chilly, wet rawness of Britain does stimulate people to keep moving and working. Activities such as study, research and reading seem easier to do on a cold, rainy day in Britain than on a gorgeous, warm, sunny day in the Southwest of the United States.

Finally, the climate does yield a very few exceptional days when it seems that there is no more wonderful place in the whole world to be than in Britain. Fortunately, these days do happen during the height of the tourist season. Some of these days are thick and moist and gray, when one can sense the heavy richness of life everywhere. Then there are those warm days when the sun is radiant and all of nature simply bursts in rich color and scent to the extent that it almost overwhelms. Perhaps one such day is really worth two dozen miserable, rainy weekend afternoons. Perhaps the rarity of such lovely days makes them all the more appreciated, just as a glass of cool water becomes a treasure after a hike through a burning desert.

Black England and Green England

The English portion of Britain can be divided roughly into two zones. In the south and east there is an undulating well-watered, broad plain, broken now and then by a line of gentle, green hills; in the west and north of England, rough, broken country predominates, with parts of it forming well-worn mountain ranges.

Up until the nineteenth century, civilization was centered on the great plain because in agrarian societies the fertility of the soil, the ease of farming and the length of the growing season together determine where the population will be the most dense. Therefore, England's broad plain has had the richest history and most of the oldest towns. Ever since the industrial revolution, however, large populations have concentrated where the subsoil resources have been the most ample. Towns and cities sprang up in colder, more barren regions of England which were sparsely populated before the demand for coal and iron intensified. These places, towns like Leeds, Rochdale or Bradford, do not draw tourists. They are in "black England," replete with slag heaps, smoke, pylons and cooling towers. In general, lighter, cleaner, more modern industries — what would be called "high tech" today — tend to be developed in the south. The heavy, coal-based industries, such as steel, textiles and shipbuilding, remain in the north and west. Parts of this region can be as ugly as the desolate landscape along portions of the New Jersey Turnpike. Even so, visitors to Britain ought to see at least one of these industrial centers, just to appreciate the fact that a workaday, hardbitten England exists side by side with the quaint and beautiful land of castles, cathedrals and Tudor half timber.

Seeking Scenery in Britain

When it comes to looking at scenes of natural beauty, many Americans, particularly those from the West, are rather jaded. They have mile upon mile of celebrated and uncelebrated spectacular scenery literally in their backyards. There are little-known places in Colorado familiar to the author which would be swarmed over if they were in Europe, sites that would probably be furnished with all sorts of colorful legends and romantic names.

America is probably the best endowed country in the world when it comes to scenic areas. Britain is far behind in this category. The scenic attractions of Britain that are usually cited are the rough country and coast in Devon and Cornwall; the rough country of Yorkshire; the mountains of Wales and Scotland; and the Lake District in the northwest of England where famous poets sat about chilly shores in the drizzle. All of this put together comprises but a tiny fraction of the acres upon acres of natural beauty in the United States. Moreover, places of natural beauty in Britain always have swarms of people appreciating them to death.

Outside of these areas, and also outside of the ugly, industrial areas and suburban sprawls, there are pleasant, undulating green plains, some ridges of dark green hills and some nicely wooded spots. Everywhere the vegetation is lush, with richly scented, gorgeous flowers blooming during the warmest part of the year. All of this is very nice, but unspectacular. It is a fitting background for the old towns, cities, castles, cathedrals, museums and other historical and cultural sites that visitors should concentrate upon seeing.

Visitors should not traipse over Britain to look at scenery when so much of it abounds in America. Besides, roads, railroads, houses, shops and all other manifestations of civilization are thick almost everywhere on an island bearing such a dense population. There is nothing at all to match the Grand Canyon, the deserts of Arizona, the multicolored plateau of New Mexico, the majesty of the Rockies, the thick forest of the Great Smokies, the swampland of Florida or the brilliance of New England in early October. Let one aphorism prevail: When in Britain, seek out civilization, not nature.

THE GEOGRAPHY OF LONDON

A World City

Consideration of the geography of the most marvelous part of Britain has been saved for last. London is a world unto itself, unique and different from the rest of Britain and unique and different from the other cities of the world.

It has been said that all of Britain can be divided into two parts: London and the rest of it. Nothing in the United States can compare to London. One out of every eight persons in Britain lives within the borders of London, a fraction that would be even lower if the whole metropolitan region were taken into consideration. No American city can compare to this urban concentration; roughly only one out of thirty-three Americans lives in New York City. Moreover, London has the importance of New York, Washington, Philadelphia, Boston and everything in between all rolled into one great circular-shaped metropolis. London is the center of government, trade, finance, the arts, publishing and urban culture. One odd-sounding description that seems to fit is that London is a giant head belonging to a very small body.

London is also a world city, sharing that designation with very few other metropolitan centers. It has been argued that only New York and San Francisco fit that description in the United States. All the rest of the cities in America and Britain are more or less provincial. What makes a world city? It is being cosmopolitan in outlook and composition; having black, brown, yellow and white people sharing it; having dozens of languages spoken; and having the size, importance, and magnetism to pull in able, ambitious and energetic people from all over the world. Visitors to world cities can feel this status. The world cities seem to declare that they are true centers of human life on this planet.

Coming to Grips with London's Geography: Dividing London Up

South of the Thames
London can be divided up into four areas con-

veniently. The Thames River (pronounced Tems, with an "e" as in elephant) snakes through the metropolis, dividing off South London. South London is not particularly interesting. Some important buildings do line the southern bank of the river, such as the National Theatre and Lambeth Palace, where the Archbishop of Canterbury officially resides. The southern bank is also lined by a number of large hospitals. But sprawling southwards from the bank is a vast, grim, grimy urban area, primarily consisting of uninteresting residential blocks. After wartime destruction, large parts have been rebuilt in rather massive and stark concrete.

The East End and the City of London

North of the Thames, another division can be made between East London and West London. In the eastern part of the metropolis the City of London proper can be found, a rectangular-shaped area that hugs the Thames and at one time comprised the old, walled Roman and medieval London. Today, the City has a thriving business community reminiscent of lower Manhattan. The Bank of England, the Royal Exchange, Lloyds of London and a host of other worldwide companies have their headquarters in the City of London. The Tower of London and the new Museum of London are other attractions in the vicinity. An army of soberly dressed British businessmen descend upon the City daily, and on weekends the area can be as deserted as Wall Street at similar times.

North and east of the City is the East End proper. It is famous for its working class cockney neighborhoods. During World War II, the area was severely bombed, particularly along the port section stretching eastwards along the Thames. The scars of the Blitz are still deep, despite the massive new concrete complexes and modern buildings that have gone up. The old neighborhoods have irregular skylines because so many buildings were destroyed and have not been replaced by anything more than parking lots. Some people who did not like the prewar shabbiness of the area sometimes refer to the Blitz as urban renewal on a grand scale by the *Luftwaffe*.

The East End does have many similarities with London south of the Thames. It, too, is a vast residential area for poorer people that is largely grim, gray and relatively uninteresting. Nevertheless, there is a vast open air market along Portobello Road on Sundays that evokes the echoes of the London of Charles Dickens in its sights, sounds and, above all, characters.

The West End

The West End is a misnomer because it really comprises the heart of central London. An area has developed over the centuries that stretches for many miles to the west of the so-called West End. Nevertheless, the name "West End" has stuck from the time centuries ago when it comprised the new and fashionable part of London.

The West End has the greatest tourist attractions. It is here that the visitor will spend most of the time because so many important places are clustered together: museums, theatres, famous squares, shopping streets, Parliament and palaces. There is so much to see that a following section is taken up exclusively with getting around in this area of central London.

Greater London

London stretches in all directions from its center along the Thames. A great ring road swings in a wide circle miles from the center, and beyond this extends another wide circle consisting of a patchy green belt. A vast series of bedroom neighborhoods made up of hundreds of thousands of row houses or semi-detached houses fills greater London, making it one of the largest and most densely packed urban regions in the whole world.

Much of greater London is connected directly to the city center by the tube, or underground, which sends the spokes of its rail lines surprisingly far in all directions of the circle of population. At key underground stops, rail lines feed commuters from farther out into the greater London system. Considering all of the people and space involved, it works surprisingly well when there are no strikes.

American type suburban neighborhoods with ample lawns and yards surrounding detached, ranch style wooden or brick houses are not to be found, although occasionally a single house here and there will be comparable in everything except price. The price in Britain is astronomical.

Coming to Grips with the Geography of Central London

Newcomers to London are well advised never to go out without a handy, folding map of the center of the metropolis. Of course, people on the street will be helpful in giving directions, but some private map study really ought to be undertaken to avoid asking unnecessary questions.

The richness of a few square miles of central London is simply amazing. Getting around in this milieu is not so easy at first because the streets curve into and away from one another at odd angles and the squares and streets leading to them seem all pushed in on one another. Visitors are often confused trying to find their way from one major hub to another. "Can you tell me how to get to Leicester Square?" is a question so often heard in a broad American accent on London's streets, with variations of the question substituting Trafalgar Square and Piccadilly Circus for Leicester Square.

These three hubs seem to be the best places to begin to sort out central London's geography. The three form a roughly irregular triangle (see the diagram). Piccadilly Circus is London's Times Square, having a reputation for brassiness, loudness and crudeness. But it is much less dangerous and degenerate. Circus means a place where roads come together. Remember that Piccadilly Circus is roughly to the west of Leicester (pronounced Lester) Square. Regent Street feeds traffic into Piccadilly Circus from the northwest, and Shaftesbury Avenue brings traffic from the east.

Leicester Square is at the very heart of the theatre district. For some time, a kiosk in the middle of the square has sold discount theatre tickets for performances of the calendar day. One word of caution: An umbrella is recommended for Leicester Square, rain or shine, on account of the huge flocks of birds that splatter everything in the area. Note that the square itself is just to the west of the London underground stop of that name.

Of all the sights in the London area, Trafalgar Square is probably one of the three most memorable, along with the Tower of London and Parliament. Who can forget Nelson's column, the floodlit fountains and the great lions? Trafalgar Square is just southeast of Leicester Square via Charing Cross Road. Flanking Trafalgar Square itself are the National Gallery and the National Portrait Gallery. The Royal

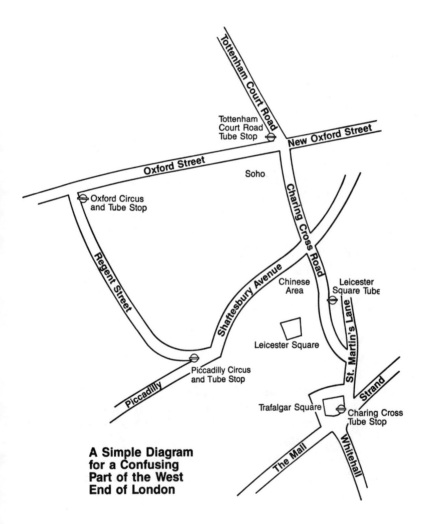

**A Simple Diagram
for a Confusing
Part of the West
End of London**

Academy is some distance, closer to Piccadilly Circus.

Trafalgar Square is an excellent departure point for the avid urban hiker. Whitehall is a great road leading directly south, past government buildings and the colorful Horse Guards to the Houses of Parliament and Westminster Abbey. The Mall is another great road that leads southwest to Buckingham Palace. The Strand is the first segment of a major street leading northeast. After a while it becomes Fleet Street, then Ludgate Hill, where it passes St. Paul's in East London, and then Canon Street, where it leads up to the monument put up after the Great Fire of 1666. The Tower of London is not far from the monument. Only heroic hikers should start out on Fleet Street for the Tower.

Many of London's other major attractions are not far away from this triangle of hubs. Running east and west, but north of these three hubs, is the busiest shopping street in all of London — Oxford Street — particularly the stretch of it between Oxford Circus and Tottenham Court Road (pronounced Totten-em). Between Oxford Street and lines drawn between Leicester Square to the east and Piccadilly Circus to the west is the Soho district, where Karl Marx once lived. Today it is a place for foreign restaurants intermingled with enterprises of all sorts dealing with pornography and commercial sex. Just up behind Trafalgar Square, towards Shaftesbury Avenue, are the densely packed streets of London's remarkable Chinatown, featuring a great number of splendid and varied Chinese restaurants.

The best way to get to and away from central London is via the tube or the underground because it is fast, direct and efficient. (See the section on Transportation for practical details on how to use the tube.)

The Tower of London will require a stop at Tower Hill station; the Houses of Parliament can best be reached from Westminster station; a whole group of museums can be reached from the South Kensington station. These include the Victoria and Albert Museum, the National History Museum, and the Science Museum. The most helpful maps of London will have the tube stops superimposed so that the visitor can know at a glance which stop to aim for. The maps of the British Tourist Authority (64 St. James's Street, London SW 1A1NF) are very good.

SIGNIFICANT ASPECTS OF THE BRITISH ECONOMY

Why Britain Is Preoccupied with Economic Concerns

The worrisome state of the British economy is a topic that seems to preoccupy Britons constantly. They maintain a perpetual gloominess about the economy, a pessimism not unlike their reaction to the weather. Someone observed that the British worry as much about economic matters as Americans worry about sex!

There are some very good reasons underlying Britons' grave concern over the fate of their economy. Size is a key factor. Britain's small, densely populated island simply does not have enough farmland to feed everyone. Therefore, at least a third of the food consumed in Britain must come from abroad. A stroll through the shops of any high street (main street in America) reveals food products from all sorts of places — New Zealand, Australia, Israel, Spain, France, the United States and Canada. British farms often specialize in producing high quality and expensive dairy, meat, fruit and vegetable crops, leaving the production of basic staples to those countries that have the vast acreage to grow them cheaply. Canadian or American wheat, for instance, has been cheaper than locally grown wheat in Britain since the 1870s. Much British land is given over to pasture, taking advantage of the lushness of plant growth to raise animals for wool and food. If plowed, much of this land could produce good crops, but the labor and investment for such crops would be too costly in most cases.

America stands in sharp contrast as a food producer. It has a huge agricultural hinterland, a population spread more thinly across our landscape, substantial agricultural exports and surplus agricultural products bulging out of storage facilities.

The American situation in regard to raw materials is also highly advantageous in comparison to Britain. The United States has an abundance of most of the basic materials needed in an industrial age, and what the nation does not have can be imported readily as a result of the power of the American economic system. By contrast, Britain is short of all kinds of raw materials. Britain's coal and iron mines once led the world in production, but the best has long been taken out of them. The list of raw materials that Britain must import in quantity is long, and includes timber, various fibers and many kinds of metal and metal ores.

Petroleum is an exception to this picture. The United States must import a high percentage of the petroleum it uses, even though it is the second greatest crude oil producer in the world, second only to the Soviet Union. A recent blessing for the British economy has come from the seemingly providential find of ample oil deposits under the North Sea.

Without this North Sea oil, dependence upon imported oil would have been disastrous to the British economy. Although the oil pumped from the North Sea is low grade, Britain has become a net exporter of petroleum. Nevertheless, this fact is hardly reflected at British gas pumps, where the prices have remained breathtakingly high in recent years.

How does the British economy pay for these imports of food and raw materials? Britain manages to survive by living on brains and skills that are applied to producing goods and services to meet overseas demand. In addition, many British firms are involved in banking, shipping and insurance services. The profits turned on such services can be used, eventually, to purchase food and raw materials. These are the so-called "invisible exports" of the economy. Many firms manufacture finished products from imported raw materials and semi-processed goods. Substantial quantities of these finished goods are then exported, thereby earning profit which can be applied to importing more raw materials and foodstuffs. This never ending cycle of services, exports and imports keeps the economy of this crowded island going.

Britain has an elaborately developed infrastructure suited for this economic activity. An elaborate financial network is superimposed on an old but workable system of docks, rails and trucking. A skilled work force with considerable technical and managerial expertise operates a series of factory complexes that range from the near obsolete to the ultramodern. Despite all of the complaints about the British economy, its level of development is quite high.

Given an economy that depends on its brains, skills and exports, the balance of payments question is crucial for Britain. The balance of payments measures exports against imports and registers either a surplus or a deficit. The American balance of payments situation, although it has shown disturbing deficits in recent years, is a far less critical measurement for the economy overall than it is in Britain, for a very good reason. The United States has vast and diverse areas that are highly productive in agriculture, manufacturing and in producing various raw materials. Huge amounts of goods, services and foodstuffs are produced and traded at home in a gigantic internal market. Americans spend most of their economic energy producing for this internal market, and they consume most of the products from it. This makes foreign trade relatively less important than it is for a country such as Britain. Americans do not have to agonize over the balance of payments the way Britons do because it is not such an absolutely critical economic indicator for the United States.

The British economy can be compared to the American economy overall by the analogy of two baseball players going to bat. The first begins with an automatic count of two strikes against him; the second begins with an automatic count of three balls and no strikes. Britain's precarious economy will continue to face crises which are basically attributable to Britain's geography and demography, and not to the policies of any particular government nor to any particular Prime Minister nor to the socialist component in the system.

Understanding British Socialism

Americans hear and read many peculiar, contradictory and often confusing things about the socialist component of Britain's economy. Socialism is a specter, or haunting phenomenon, for many Americans because the term is usually employed in a pejorative manner in the United States. Socialism conjures up images of arbitrary rule, lack of freedom and rigid controls. Many Americans wrongly use the term interchangeably with communism, a term that can link socialism with all sorts of frightening images, including Stalin's mad purges, state censorship and Siberian prison camps.

Europeans are generally more sophisticated than Americans about the meaning and implications of modern socialism. First of all, modern socialism in Western Europe is not communism, nor is it a step or stage heading towards communism. Communism is a particular kind of Marxist system prevailing in the Soviet Union, Eastern Europe, China and a few scattered nations elsewhere. Western European socialism differs in many ways from the communism found in these countries. Perhaps the most important difference is that Western European socialism is wedded to the democratic ballot box. This means that if a majority of people in any country wish to dismantle some or all of what is socialistic, they may elect representatives who will do so. This is precisely what has gone on in Britain recently, as Mrs. Thatcher's Conservative government, backed by an electoral mandate, has sought to remove substantial aspects of the socialist component of the British economy.

What really prevails in Britain and in many other European nations, such as France, West Germany or Sweden, is not socialism but a mixed economy that has a strong component of socialism as well as a strong component of capitalism. Under a mixed economy, markets have both considerable regulation and considerable freedom. Most of the political issues in these countries center on what the precise formula for the economy's mix should be. Politicians debate specific issues that boil down to whether there should be a little more or a little less of the capitalistic or the socialistic component. Nobody debates the need to have a mix; this is taken for granted, even by governments as staunchly conservative as that of Mrs. Thatcher.

Just what makes up the socialistic component? There are several types of socialistic institutions and programs. Some industries are nationalized, the government's bureaucracy exercises controls over business and banking, and an elaborate welfare system exists, which includes socialized medicine. It is worthwhile to take up several of these aspects separately.

Nationalization

The nationalization of industry has long been one of the goals of the left wing movements in Europe, what they have called "socializing the means of production." The accomplishments of nationalization are a mixed picture, so that debates over whether to nationalize more enterprises or to denationalize some of them crop up regularly in British politics.

The list of nationalized industries includes railroads, telegraph, telephone, central banking, aircraft, the coal industry, the docks, British Leyland (the truck and auto manufacturer) and several other operations. Since some of these industries were already economic failures when the government stepped in to take them over, it is no wonder that the government has had difficulty in turning them around to show a profit. Detractors claim that nationalized industries are wasteful and inefficient under government management and, on the other hand, proponents claim that nationalized industries show considerable improvement after going public, especially in providing better services.

Without doubt, conservative Americans will be hostile to the concept of nationalization, but several mitigating factors ought to be borne in mind considering British nationalization, which will help dispel the image of a harsh government arbitrarily smothering private economic enterprise.

First of all, nationalization of any industry cannot take place except through open, democratic procedures. Nationalization can be duly enacted into law only after gaining the approval of a majority of the members of the House of Commons. The bureaucracy cannot nationalize anything without the express legal permission of a majority of the democratically elected members of Parliament.

Secondly, in most cases when nationalization takes place, nearly all of the managers and workers of the old private corporations show up as the managers and workers of the new public corporations. There is usually such continuity in staff and in conditions of work that most of the new employees of the state are hardly aware that nationalization has occurred.

A third mitigating factor is that management functions as a separate corporate board of directors, and is not blended into the bureaucracy. The management does have a responsibility to run the enterprise efficiently and can be held accountable. Also, in many economic activities, private competition is allowed to exist, much in the same way that the most conspicuous nationalized American activity, the Post Office, faces competition from various companies in delivering overnight letters and packages.

The Welfare State

The component of British socialism called the "welfare state" has been far less controversial in Britain than nationalization. Since it is generally highly popular with the voters, even the staunchest of Conservatives will not try to dismantle the welfare state directly. Instead, they nibble at the edges. Most British people take the welfare state for granted as a mark of a high civilization, and almost two generations have grown up since it was put into operation from 1945 to 1950. These generations have not known anything else but cradle to the grave welfare security. The system is simply regarded as normal in Britain.

The idea of a comprehensive welfare system often does not sit well with conservative Americans. For some of them, it conjures the image of lazy people flopping about, enjoying a secure, comfortable living without working for it. Some newspapers in the United States reinforce such negative images by spotlighting only the shortcomings and anomalies that crop up from time to time in the British system.

Welfare means something quite different to British people. It means that there is a safety net under everyone, just as there is a safety net under trapeze performers in the circus. Everyone is assured of having the basics to sustain life, namely food, housing, clothing, health care and education. Drastic sickness, old age and unemployment can no longer be haunting specters of financial catastrophe as they have been for all the centuries when ordinary people simply could not lay enough money aside as savings to cope with these situations. Becoming sick, old and unemployed are still unfortunate circumstances, but at least the sufferer knows that he or she will be taken care of by the community during those difficult times.

In the United States, we have something of a welfare state in existence also, although Americans are disinclined to call it that. Social Security, Medicare, Medicaid, food stamps and various entitlements all help comprise our rather patchier and less complete system. We have the persistent problem that there are always people who suffer from its inadequacies, particularly those who fall between the cracks. Another problem is that some persons and institutions are able to take advantage of benefits improperly.

Aspects of the welfare state in Britain are always subject to criticism by British people, of course, but in general it is seen as a vast public insurance system, with everyone contributing and everyone eligible to draw benefits.

British Capitalism

Despite all of the jobs and functions that the state has taken over, or collectivized, since World War II, it has been estimated that at least eight out of every ten jobs in Britain are still in the private sector, meaning that these are jobs from capitalistic activities. Indeed, much of the strength and vitality in Britain's economy comes from the flexibility and incentive of entrepreneurs who are out to make a pound, whether the pound comes from American tourists, teenage music fans, fashion-conscious wives, visiting Arabs or simply anyone who is willing to spend. In considering the more spectacularly profitable breakthroughs in British popular culture since World War II, it is quite clear that no government direction could ever have developed and marketed the Beatles or the mini-skirt. The same can be said for many non-glamorous breakthroughs in science and technology in recent years.

The capitalistic endeavors that made Britain such a power in the Victorian era live on in the mixed economy. Famous British firms still operate worldwide, and British resources of people, money and managing give strength to a diverse range of multinational corporations. The City of London remains one of the world's great centers of high finance, ranking with Wall Street, Hong Kong and Singapore. The City is still noted for its speed, power and skilled professionalism.

Admirers of the British economic system claim that the best of capitalism is kept and that its most negative features of tooth and claw are removed or ameliorated by the mix of socialism in the economy. It is a contention worth pondering.

The National Health Service

The existence of British socialized medicine, called the National Health Service, is one of the significant differences with the United States. Since it is controversial on both sides of the Atlantic, some consideration of its operation is in order.

First of all, tourists who become ill or have an accident in Britain will be treated by the National Health Service without cost. Special insurance is unnecessary in Britain. In general, emergency services are quite good. Medics and ambulances can be counted upon for promptness and efficiency.

The more negative features of National Health will be encountered by long-term visitors who have medical problems that are not particularly urgent. Under these circumstances, British National Health will most likely seem frustrating on account of its delays, and it will allow invidious comparisons to be made with the fast, elaborate and expensive health care that the middle classes in America have come to expect. Visitors have a way out, however, which is opting for private care. Increasingly over recent years, more and more physicians have decided to put more of their time or all of their time into private practice. There are also numerous private hospitals alongside the public hospitals. So for a good fee, anyone in Britain, tourist or resident, can go to the head of the line (or queue) and receive rather good treatment.

What really exists in British medicine are two competing and overlaid systems of medicine, one private and one public, one for the affluent and one for the poorer members of society. It is, in fact, a duplication of the competing and overlaid systems of public and private education. As in education, the private care sector has gained a reputation for being better. On the other hand, National Health and the state schools are what the less fortunate have to put up with. Clearly, the emergence of this dual system was certainly not what the architects of the welfare state had envisioned.

Everyone who has spent some time in Britain has either heard or experienced at least one or two genuine horror stories about the National Health Service. The standard themes involve incredibly long waits, crowded conditions, bungled operations and incompetent doctors or dentists. Many stories feature foreign medical personnel, usually Indian or Pakistani, who have such difficulty with English that it frightens the patients or causes a mistake in the treatment. Such stories, when taken together, do point up a fundamental shortcoming of National Health: the system tried to do too much too fast with inadequate resources.

There are simply not enough doctors, dentists or medical facilities to go around to accomplish all of the ambitious tasks that the National Health Service has claimed as its responsibilities. At the outset, all persons in Britain were to receive free medical care, dental care, hospitalization, psychiatric services, prescriptions and even eyeglasses and dentures. These provisions were all too ambitious, so eventually various fees and partial payments had to be imposed for many of these services.

Yet even when all of the failures, shortcomings and horror tales about the National Health Service are taken into account, its striking achievements cannot be denied. For centuries, the majority of ordinary people in Britain were chronically deprived of basic health care. Vast numbers needed dentures or eyeglasses, or suffered regularly from some painful chronic malady, or had a health impediment that could have been corrected by treatment. This sad state of health was revealed when men were called up for the draft during the World Wars of this century, and a high percentage were found unfit for military service. Other statistics on life expectancy and the recurrence of epidemics also reflected the low standard of medical services available to the masses of Britain before the National Health Service was instituted.

There have been dramatic improvements all along the line since National Health's ambitious programs have gotten underway. Much of the effort has been prophylactic, involving the regular screening of categories of people, such as children and underground miners. Despite the frequent delays, frustrations, overcrowding and understaffing, the ordinary Briton does appreciate the fact that he or she has free medical service that is at least generally adequate most of the time. These Britons know that they are on a particular doctor's list of patients, and that they can see their doctor when needed. In turn, the doctor knows that he receives a fee for each of the patients on his roster, whether they need to see him or not. Compared to what ordinary and poorer Britons had before National Health, the system is still a substantial improvement. The only fair way to view socialized medicine is in this historic perspective.

The British National Health Service and American Medicine

Unfortunately, many comparisons are made between the high-powered health care industry in the United States and British National Health without taking the British historical perspective into account. These comparisons contribute to the negative attitude that most American physicians and dentists have towards socialized medicine. They fear for their status and economic rewards. Of course, most American doctors and dentists are very well trained and work very hard at their professions. In many cases, their strenuous workdays preclude serious reading outside of their specialties, leaving them less informed on social and political matters than they should be. Therein might lie the reason for their professions' opposition to the principles of socialized medicine.

In America, medicine remains one of the best fields for a poor but very bright young person to enter in order to gain a good living quickly. In the right location with the right specialty, a doctor can become wealthy, if he or she invests wisely. British doctors are paid much less than American doctors, but nevertheless most of them stay in Britain instead of emigrating for higher salaries. Under a socialized system, average American doctors would probably receive less remuneration, possibly quite a bit less.

In Britain, medical doctors are not only paid less, but they also seem to have a less exalted status than American doctors. They are professionals similar in social esteem to engineers, clergymen and lawyers. The adulation that many American doctors receive in their communities does not seem to prevail in Britain. On the other hand, there are fewer malpractice suits.

American doctors and dentists should never lose sight of the fact that their counterparts in the British system have the option to continue private practice if they wish. They should also recognize that National Health is for the most part run by doctors and dentists themselves. They sit on the boards, committees and commissions, and draw up the rules touching upon medical matters. They are the ones responsible for supervising, designing and disciplining the system within the limits of the resources available. If American medicine takes major steps towards socialized medicine in the future, doctors and dentists will undoubtedly be in charge of the new arrangements.

Perhaps a trend in this direction is well under way in America, judging by the piecemeal additions to Medicare and Medicaid responsibilities in recent years. Perhaps this will lead to greater equalization of the quality of health care in America in the future.

CHAPTER THREE

Understanding Aspects of British Culture

LANGUAGE

The Queen's English and the American Dialect

English certainly has come close to becoming the new international language, a status that only Latin once enjoyed in our civilization. Of all the hundreds of millions who speak English around the globe, it is impossible to tell just how many speak British English rather than the American dialect of English. Most Americans are not accustomed to having their language labeled a dialect, but by some definitions of language, that is exactly how it can be categorized. Of the parts of the world that emerged from the old British Empire, only Canada speaks American English. All of the other places throughout the world once under the British flag speak British English, sometimes with a particular local accent. Included are India, Malaya, Hong Kong, Nigeria, Kenya, Jamaica, Australia, New Zealand to name but a few. American English shows up around the world among those who speak English as a second language, often because American businesses and military installations are so widespread. There are also countless thousands who speak American English because they studied in the United States. Nevertheless, in many quarters there is a consensus that British English is better English, a prejudice shared by quite a few Americans. In Britain it is a conviction.

The Importance of Language in Britain

Just how a person says something means much more in Britain than it does in the United States. Listeners are keenly attuned to pronunciation and vocabulary because in Britain speech is one of the best indicators to use in placing people within the categories of the pervasive class system. Unlike English in the United States, there is only one proper way to speak the language in Britain. Proper English can be heard on the BBC, in private school instruction, at the universities and in the mouths of properly educated persons all the way up to the Prime Minister and to the royal family itself. All other accents, all regional dialects and all use of slang are deemed below-standard English. Aspiring upwardly mobile persons pursuing various careers often become terribly frustrated in the attempt to keep from speaking the way they spoke at home and in their inferior schools. British ears are so keen that they can detect a person's educational background, no matter how hard he or she may work to contrive a "proper" accent.

Not everyone in Britain wishes to speak standard English. Scots, for instance, take great pride in their dialect, to the extent that they have insisted that the local BBC carry programs and employ announcers using the Scots dialect. Lower class Londoners enjoy their Cockney speech, rich in fast, amusing slang. People in the north of England feel that a person's ordinary, warm, decent qualities are revealed in the use of the local dialect. Visitors get a taste of this when bus conductors taking the fare say "ta" for "thanks" and call the passengers of the opposite sex "love." To these people and others who do not want to speak it, "proper" English usually connotes artificiality and snobbishness. For many it is the sound of people who have money, privilege and coldness.

How Americans Escape Language Snobbery in Britain

One of the worst aspects of British society is how speech can bring on painful self-consciousness for some people and deft snobbery on the part of others. The strained self-consciousness that British people experience in using their language enables the American visitor to appreciate the generally free and easy tolerance of language usage at home. Fortunately, Americans in Britain are free from this British game because they stand outside of British class relationships, a position guaranteed by their American dialect. Even so, language can put Americans in embarrassing situations. Saying the wrong word or mispronouncing a word might draw mild criticism or mild amusement from such people as shop attendants. For instance, "pants" in American means "underpants" in Britain, where pants are "trousers." "Tomato" pronounced "ā" instead of "ah" is conspicuous in a British restaurant or grocery. But no American will suffer to have his or her education, social standing and family background quickly assessed by the spoken word.

The use of American English in Britain has a bright side. British people generally enjoy talking with Americans who are inclined to speak without inhibitions. Also, American English is the dialect used in much of imported light entertainment, and it is also the dialect used in carrying out many feats of high technology, such as space exploration, that British people admire so greatly. Regional variations of American English are also appreciated in Britain. Southern or Texas pronunciations are relished. Overall, the American visitor has a great advantage in that dialect and slang provide a ready topic for initiating conversations in Britain.

In a way, it is unfortunate that the New England accent was not selected as the standard speech for announcers when radio was developed in the United States. The bland Middle Western sound was selected instead, largely because it was the most neutral of all the American regions. Had the New England pronunciations become standard through use on the media, American English and British English would be much closer today.

Despite this, the sheer size of the United States guarantees that regional accents will flourish. Even American presidents have had strong regional accents, as the speeches of John Kennedy, Lyndon Johnson and Jimmy Carter testify. By contrast, it is difficult for a British politician to carry distinct, non-standard English into high office, unless he or she comes from the

Labour Party's left or from Scotland.

Some Necessary Translations from British to American

Vocabulary in Britain and America has diverged ever since the Jamestown settlement in the early seventeenth century. Today a rich variety of words, standard and slang, appear exclusively on one or the other side of the Atlantic. While it is often amusing to discover differences in vocabulary on the spot, visitors are best forewarned and forearmed by studying the lists of translations that follow. These terms will also be useful for persons interested in British theatre, literature and journalism.

Some lists of translated words appear elsewhere in this book. See the section on Transportation for automotive terms. The section on Food has its own list, as does the section on Education. Under Medieval Britain, a list of helpful words for understanding cathedrals is included.

The words that follow have been grouped into these categories: cultural terms; very practical terms; and potentially embarrassing words and phrases. The cultural terms will certainly help in reading newspapers. They include terms pertaining to religion, politics and geography. The practical terms are for day-to-day living in Britain, and the potentially embarrassing words and phrases are some of those verbal quagmires and pitfalls that exist whenever translations are attempted.

Cultural Terms

Anglican — The Anglican Church is the Church of England. It is similar to the Episcopalian Church in

America, but it is the established, official state church in England.

Backbencher — The ordinary members of a political party, or the rank and file, sit on the back benches in Parliament.

Barrister — A barrister is a lawyer who pleads cases in court. Ordinary legal paperwork and minor business are handled by a *solicitor* in Britain.

Billion — A billion is a million million in Britain. The American billion is expressed as a thousand million.

Boxing Day — This is the holiday the day after Christmas, December 26, a time when many people give presents. The name comes from the old custom of giving boxes of presents to those owed gratuities, such as the postman.

Britain — The island which includes England, Scotland and Wales.

Brit — a slang abbreviation for British.

British — Any person or phenomenon from England, Scotland, Wales and Northern Ireland can properly be called British. A person can be, for example, Scottish and British, but never Scottish and English.

C. of E. — These initials refer to the Church of England, the Anglican Church which is established as the official state church. In worship, it is similar to the Episcopalian Church in America.

Celsius — term used officially for the temperature. Fahrenheit is used in the United States in general. 0° Celsius is the same as 32° Fahrenheit; 100° Celsius is the same as 212° Fahrenheit, the boiling point of water.

Chapel — a religious meetinghouse or church for members of Nonconformist or Non-Anglican Protestant denominations.

Circus — a place where important streets inter-sect. Piccadilly Circus and Oxford Circus are examples.

City — "The City" means the old City of London, now a square mile comprising London's financial district.

Cockney — This noun or adjective refers to working class East London culture and the accent that goes with it. Loosely, it can mean a working class Londoner.

Continent — This term British people use to describe the rest of Europe.

Corporation — This term means municipal government, what is called local government in many parts of the United States. The American word "corporation" means "limited company" in Britain, abbreviated "Ltd."

Council House or *Flat* — refers to subsidized public housing.

Demo — This is a popular abbreviation for demonstration.

Dole — These are welfare payments, usually to unemployed persons. "On the dole" usually means chronically unemployed.

East Anglia — This is the eastern hump on the map of England, a rather flat plain.

East End — This is the working class, Cockney, part of London.

Fleet Street — This is the street in London that is noted for journalism.

Free Churches — This is another name for the Nonconformist Churches, those that are Protestant but do not conform to the established Church of England.

Football — The American game of soccer is called

football in Britain, where it is immensely popular. American football, rarely played, is called just that.

Guy Fawkes Night — is a carnival night of bonfires and fireworks on November 5. Children beg as they do in the United States on Halloween. It commemorates the capture of Guy Fawkes, who tried to blow up the king and the legislature early in the seventeenth century.

High Church — A tendency in the Anglican Church to stress liturgy, communion and the rich history of the church. Its opposite is the *low church* movement, which stresses simplicity and piety.

Holiday — This word is used in Britain for "vacation." On holiday means on vacation.

Home Office — The Home Office is the government department responsible for law and order, domestic affairs and immigration.

Hustings — These are election meetings. The term formerly meant a platform candidates literally stood upon. It is always used in the plural.

Life Peer — A Life Peer is a new nobleman who can sit in the House of Lords but cannot pass on the noble title. This new form of nobility was created in the 1950s.

Limited Company — This is the British name for a corporation, abbreviated as Ltd., just as American corporations have "Inc."

Low Church — In the Anglican Church, low church places emphasis on simplicity, piety and the Bible rather than on the rich historical traditions of the church.

Ltd. — This is the abbreviation for Limited Company, what is a corporation in America.

Mate — means friend or pal. It is a working class colloquialism.

Midlands — comprise the counties of England that are in the middle of the country, consisting of undulating plains farthest from the sea.

M.P. — This is an abbreviation for member of Parliament, the equivalent of Congressman.

Navvy — A navvy is an unskilled day laborer, originally canal and railroad builders. The term is often applied to road construction crews today.

Nonconformist — This term refers to Protestant denominations which do not conform to the Church of England, including Baptists, Congregationalists and Methodists.

P.M. — This is the abbreviation for the Prime Minister.

Provinces — This term refers to all of England outside of London.

Redundant — This odd-sounding term means being unemployed. The number of redundancies refers to the number unemployed.

Rugby — This is a game somewhat like American football. It is also called "rugger."

Rural Dean — This is a Church of England clergyman with authority over several parishes.

Scottish — This adjective is preferred to Scotch because Scotch refers to a drink, although this drink is called "whiskey" in Britain. A person from Scotland is called simply a "Scot."

Send Down — This means to expel or suspend a person from a university.

Soho — This district in central London was once known for foreigners and prostitution. It still has this reputation, but it is less dangerous and more quaint today.

Scotland Yard — This is the headquarters for London's Metropolitan Police.

Shadow Cabinet — The political party out of office has a potential cabinet formed for the time when it will return. Opposition party leaders comprise this shadow cabinet.

Solicitor — Britain has two kinds of legal professionals. Solicitors do ordinary legal work, much of it paperwork. The barristers plead cases in court.

Stalls — This term refers to theatre seats on the ground floor.

Stand for Office — In Britain, politicians stand for office; in America, politicians run for office.

T.U.C. — This is an abbreviation for the Trades Union Congress, an organization of Britain's powerful unions.

Vicar — This is the name for a Church of England parish clergyman.

West Country — This refers to the southwestern part of England, the long peninsula pointing out into the Atlantic containing Devon and Cornwall.

West End — This fashionable and rich part of London is now in the geographic center, but the historic name is retained.

Westminster — Parliament and the government are situated in this area along the Thames west of the City of London.

Whitehall — This is a street housing most of the main ministries that runs from Trafalgar Square down to Parliament. The residence of the Prime Minister is just off of it.

Work to Rule — Unions apply this to slow up and disrupt activity by rigidly adhering to rules and regulations.

Very Practical Terms

Here are quick translations of a wide range of

words, including some useful for shopping, seeking housing, or even locating a toilet.

Advert — is the British abbreviation for advertisement. Ours is "ad."

Bank Holiday — This is a day when the banks are closed and almost everything else. They occur on certain days and around other holidays.

Bathe — as a verb, means to go for a swim, not to have a bath.

Bathroom — Literally, a room where people bathe. Americans curiously use it as a euphemism for toilet, because we usually have toilets in our bathrooms. European homes and hotels usually do not.

Bed Sitter or *Bed Sit* — refers to a room that serves as a living room and a sleeping room.

Book — To book means to reserve.

Camp Bed — what Americans call a cot.

Carriage — the word for railway or subway car.

Chemist — druggist.

Chemist's Shop — drugstore, but it sells a narrower range of products than the American drugstore.

Chit — a pass or document or any piece of paper with significant writing on it can be called this.

Constable — the proper term for policeman. The Chief of Police is Chief Constable. Constable is abbreviated P.C.

Convenience — a polite term for toilet, often meaning a public toilet.

Cot — a bed for a small child. What Americans call a cot is a camp bed in Britain.

Deposit Account — a savings account.

Detached — means a house standing without being joined to another. Semi-detached is more ordinary, meaning attached on one side but not the other.

Directory Enquiries — telephone information.

Dressing Gown — means bathrobe.

Dust Bin — trash bin.

Dustman — garbage collector.

Elastic Band — rubber band.

Flat — apartment.

Fortnight — two weeks.

Full Stop — period.

Goods Lift — freight elevator.

Goods Lorry — a truck carrying freight.

Goods Train — a freight train.

G.P.O. — the General Post Office.

Greengrocer — the shop that sells fruits and vegetables, but not other staples.

High Street — The high street of a town or a district is the equivalent of "main street."

High Tea — a late afternoon meal.

Hire Purchase — the installment plan.

Hoover — a vacuum cleaner, whether it is a Hoover or any other brand. To hoover means to vacuum.

Left Luggage — a checkroom.

Lift — elevator.

Lip Balm — chap stick.

Loo — a genteel phrase for toilet, but colloquial.

Mackintosh or *Mac* — a raincoat.

Maisonette — a duplex apartment, often part of a house.

Mews — usually an old alley that has become quaint or fashionable.

P.C. — The abbreviation means Police Constable, or policeman. In print, the initials P.C. come before the name of the policeman.

Plimsols — canvas shoes or what Americans would call track shoes or, to the amusement of the British, sneakers.

Point or *Power Point* — an electrical outlet.

Queue — line.

Quid — a slang word for pound, just as "buck" is slang for dollar.

Return — a round-trip ticket.

Ring Up — to telephone.

Scent — perfume.

Semi-Detached — a term referring to a house that is attached to another house on one side but not on the other.

Service Flat — an apartment which is cleaned and serviced.

Single — a one-way ticket.

Stone — a measurement of weight that is 14 pounds. "He weighs ten stone" means that he weighs 140 pounds.

Subway — an underground passage for a busy road. What we call the subway is the underground or the tube.

Surgery — This is the medical doctor's office. It also means when the doctor is in to see his patients.

Ta — This is the familiar working class thank you.

Tea — A middle and upper class mid-afternoon snack. For the working class, tea means the meal the working man has when he comes home.

Terrace — a row of houses joined together.

Terrace House — one of the houses in a row of houses joined together.

Ton — This is 2,240 lbs. in Britain. An American ton of 2,000 lbs. is often called a short ton.

Top of the Street — the end of the street.

Torch — means flashlight.

Tower Block — means a high-rise apartment building.

Trunk Call — a long-distance phone call.

Tube — slang for the underground railway, what we would call the subway.

Turf Accountant — a bookmaker.

Underground — the underground railway, which we call the subway.

Utility — means something that is simple and cheap. The American term is "generic."

V.A.T. — This is the value added tax, which functions like a sales tax. It is often wise to ask whether it is included.

Wellingtons or Wellies — a high, waterproof British boot, similar to galoshes.

W.C. — An abbreviation for water closet that really means toilet. It is used internationally.

Zed — what the British call "Z."

Potentially Embarrassing Terms

Translations between American English and British English can involve some awkward or embarrassing misconstruing, as the following terms show:

Bill — used in place of our word "check" in places such as restaurants.

Bloke — means fellow or guy. It may not sound as innocuous to Americans as to Britons.

Bloody — a term of exasperation or annoyance. Its origin was in a curse, "God's blood."

Braces — the British word for suspenders. In Britain, suspenders mean garters.

Check — Our use of this word for bill in such places as restaurants is not followed in Britain. They say "bill."

Common — This word does not mean ordinary. It means lower class, often pejoratively.

Fag — means cigarette and sometimes a dreary

task. It is not a British slang word for homosexual. Nancy, nancy boy, pouf or queer are used in Britain.

First Floor — is really the second floor in America. What Americans call the first floor is the ground floor in Britain.

Ill — the word used instead of the American word "sick." "Sick" in Britain means nauseous, and to "be sick" means to vomit.

Keep Your Pecker Up — a classic phrase. It means "keep your spirits up" in Britain and quite another thing in America.

Knickers — an archaic term for underpants, something like bloomers in America.

Knock Up — This verb means to look up someone or wake up someone instead of slang for impregnating someone.

Mick — a colloquial and often derogatory phrase for Irishman. It is not advisable to use it.

Mr. — Oddly enough, higher ranking doctors and dentists in Britain have the title of Mr. instead of Dr. Americans often mistakenly think that they are lower ranking professionals.

Nancy or *Nancy Boy* — British slang terms for homosexual. Also pouf or queer.

Nappy — This is the British word for diaper.

Nipple — In Britain, this term is used just for part of the breast. The word "teat" refers to the nipple on a baby's bottle.

Paddy — a colloquial phrase for Irishman.

Pants — are underpants in Britain. The word "trousers" is used for our word pants.

Pouf — British slang for homosexual.

Public Bar — This is the part of the bar used by ordinary people. The slightly costlier saloon bar is supposed to be used by visitors and ladies.

Queer — means feeling unwell or queasy. It can also be slang for homosexual, as in the United States.

Rubber — an eraser and not, as in America, slang for condom.

Ruddy — a polite euphemism for bloody. It is used regularly as an adjective for nearly everything, often by very proper people.

Saloon Bar — This is the section of a bar that is somewhat better furnished where drinks cost just a little more. Visitors and women are traditionally expected to be served there instead of the public bar, where ordinary local men drink.

Sanitary Towel — the British expression for sanitary napkin.

Scent — the British word for perfume.

Screw — slang for salary in Britain.

Sick — means nauseous and to "be sick" means to vomit. The word "ill" is used in Britain for everything else.

Sticky Wicket — refers to a difficult situation and comes from a sporting expression.

Suspenders — the British word for garters. In Britain, braces mean suspenders.

Teat — This is a nipple on a baby's bottle. The term "nipple" is used exclusively for part of the breast.

Through — In a phone conversation, this means connected, not finished. When the operator asks, "Are you through?" this means "Are you connected?"

Vest — means undershirt in Britain. The American "vest" is a "waistcoat" in Britain.

Waistcoat — This means "vest" in America.

Wog — a very nasty term for a nonwhite person. It is supposed to come from an acronym for "wiley oriental gentleman" and is a term of prejudice.

EDUCATION

Contrasts with American Education

Education in Britain differs in several significant ways from education in the United States. It tends to be less democratic, more elitist and more demanding. The end result is that a thinner stream of well-educated youth go to the universities and the prestigious careers beyond.

It is generally stressed in Britain that the teachers are the professionals and the parents are mere amateurs. Therefore, the teachers run the show and the parents take advice. The author's children went to a school in London that had a sign near the entrance that read: "No parents beyond this point." The comparative lack of parental power over the schools may be attributed to the fact that Britain has weak counterparts to match the strong community influence in America expressed through school boards, Parent-Teacher Organizations and Parent Advisory Boards.

In Britain, there has long been clear emphasis on hard work in school, which is carried on over a longer school year than in America. Elementary school starts at an earlier age: Infant school takes in children five and six and lasts for two years. The British equivalent of kindergarten is far more vigorous, offering far less in the way of fun and games.

Throughout the British system, emphasis is on segregating the academically able into separate streams or into different schools. Long, grueling tests are the means used. The process reaches a culmination at the end of what Americans would call the high school years. At fifteen and sixteen, a battery of tests called the "O Levels" must be faced, and those who wish to go on to college must pass the dreaded "A Levels," usually taken in three subjects. Defenders of the British testing system say that it provides a fair screening because any pupil of whatever socio-economic background can take them. Poor but highly talented youth who do well on tests are given scholarships to the best schools. Detractors of the system say that the tests favor the upper and middle classes because the questions and material have a class bias. While admitting that brilliant working class youngsters can get a free ride to the top in education, critics maintain that the merely good working class pupils are discriminated against. The class issue flares forth in debates over education as much as racial issues have in the United States.

Two parallel systems of education operate in Britain, one public and one private. What invariably confuses Americans is that private schools are usually called "public" schools. At the time they were originally founded, usually hundreds of years ago, they were open to the general public, which really meant that they were open to the parents who were able and willing to pay the substantial fees. Eton, Harrow, Winchester and Rugby are examples of these private "public" schools. From their inception until the present, most "public" school students have been the sons of the wealthy and influential. Other private schools exist for boys and girls down to the school entering age, and most have colorful school uniforms. Costs are considerable, but parents who put a premium on their youngsters' education see the expense of tuition, and, later on, room and board, much in the same way that American parents regard the costs of college, as heavy but necessary burdens.

In most places in America, the public school gathers in almost all of the students, the good, bad and in-different. Public schools vary considerably in quality, ranging from first class, well-financed, suburban education palaces to dreary, rundown, underfinanced inner city schools to bucolic, rural-centered schools that draw students from amazing distances. There are some exceptions to the dominance of the public schools in the United States, and the scope of private education may grow in the future. For many wealthy and sophisticated parents living along the urban East Coast, competition exists to get even the youngest children into the "right" or the "best" private schools. The Roman Catholic parochial school system continues on, and there are many Bible-based fundamentalist and other religious schools, as well as so-called "white academies" that have been spawned by desegregation and busing. Military schools and "prep" schools have long traditions in America. Yet when all of these exceptions are considered together, they do not add up to a parallel system of private education such as that in Britain. The norm for most American students remains kindergarten to the twelfth grade in the public school system.

Sorting Out the British Educational System

For American parents who plan to send their children to British schools or for university students who plan to study in Britain or simply for students who will encounter their British counterparts, it helps to sort out the confusing British educational system and understand the terms used.

At the Elementary Level
Primary School is what we call "grade school," and

it goes until age eleven. *Infant School* takes up the first two years of primary school, and is attended by pupils five to six years old. This is followed by *Junior School,* the part of primary school that educates youngsters from seven until eleven. Parallel to the primary school is the *Prep School,* or *Preparatory School,* which is a private school for the elementary school having high status. Many take both boys and girls up to age thirteen.

At the Junior High and High School Levels

The most prestigious schools, academically and socially, are the so-called *Public Schools,* which are, as mentioned, mainly old and famous private boarding schools, including Eton, Harrow, Rugby and Winchester. They take boys from ages thirteen to the time they are ready to enter the universities. Some schools take girls of the same ages, but public schools in Britain are rarely co-educational and rarely non-boarding. Parents of most public school students see their teenagers only on holidays, what Americans call vacations. The social connections fostered at these ancient, traditional public schools are of considerable importance to the nation's elite. The "old school tie" leads to advantages in politics, business and the professions.

Public school pupils learn much else besides academic subjects. The emphasis on community living and sports provides lessons in sportsmanship, friendship, authority, loyalty and team play. In many schools, there is an atmosphere of a rather muscular, cold water Christianity. Recently, the defenders of the public schools have become embattled with members of the left wing of the Labour party who want to close them down because they perceive them as bastions of privilege.

Only a very small fraction of the population attends these famous so-called "public schools." The rest go to day schools, either private or public in the American sense. Even the state-supported schools in Britain tend to segregate the more able from the less able students. *Grammar Schools* are academically oriented, take in high achieving students and have a span equivalent to our sixth to twelfth grades. Grammar school students are given much hard work in preparation for the universities and their careers beyond.

The *Secondary Modern School* takes in the less academically talented, in general, and has a span equivalent to the American sixth to twelfth grades. Practical subjects are encouraged, since students are not expected to go to the university. Moreover, many are seen as potential school drop-outs, teenagers who will swell the horde of very young employees seen all over Britain working at low paying jobs that offer little hope for advancement in the future. Youngsters indulging in extreme fashions are likely to come from this group, probably to compensate for their bleak prospects.

In recent years, there has been an attempt to get away from strict segregation into streams of academically able and less able students. The *Comprehensive School* has been the result of this move towards the American way of education. Students of varying talents enter them.

At the University Level

British universities can be divided into three categories. The foremost universities are Oxford and Cambridge, comparable to Harvard and Yale in prestige and world renown. Both universities were founded in the Middle Ages and display rich architecture dating back over the centuries. The term "Oxbridge" is used to refer to both schools as a single entity, much as Americans would say "Ivy League" to indicate a certain group of prestigious East Coast universities. Next are the "red brick" universities, solid, older universities, many of them founded in the nineteenth century when bricks were the usual building material. Some of them, such as the University of Manchester or the University of Birmingham, are institutions of high reputation, particularly in some of their specialties. Finally, a number of ultra-modern universities sprouted after World War II, sometimes called "cement block and plate glass universities." They resemble many campuses in the American West, and have few traditions in a nation that relishes tradition.

There are some sharp contrasts between British universities and their American counterparts. First of all, the student population is selected from around 17 percent of the population of university age. American universities and colleges draw close to 40 percent of that age group. The more selective British students bring a solid grounding in basic academic subjects with them. Such subjects as driver education, journalism, theatre, gymnastics and band do not take up very much time during their college preparatory years. Therefore, college instruction can begin at a more advanced level and continue in a narrower, more specialized and intense manner. By contrast, American university education is broader and more diverse, and American students have more opportunities to pick and choose from a variety of subjects. Another contrast is that most British undergraduate degrees take only three years to acquire.

In general, British universities emphasize closer relations with junior faculty, called *tutors*, who give *tu-*

torials, which are small classes where intensive one-on-one instruction occurs. Absent is the great American obsession with regular exams, grades and grade points. In fact, the major examinations come after students are through with their undergraduate courses. A whole battery of exams at the end of college determines whether or not candidates will graduate, and they almost invariably do, and whether or not they will gain first or second class honors, which is similar to graduating *summa* or *magna cum laude* at an American university. Gaining a *first* in a chosen field is widely regarded as a splendid achievement in Britain.

The internal structure of a typical older British university is different from an American counterpart. The use of the word "college" is at the heart of the difference. At American universities, colleges denote specialized areas of instruction, such as a college of engineering or a college of natural sciences. In Britain, a college is a relatively self-contained unit, possessing its own varied student body, its own housing, its own administration and its own faculty. The offerings usually cover a wide spectrum. The university consists of a number of these colleges, but it can also offer a large library or special pieces of expensive equipment for students from any college. The advantages of both smallness and largeness are effectively combined in the British university system.

Many schools unconnected to any university have the name of "college" in Britain. Usually they are places without high status and unable to award higher degrees.

Faculty rank in Britain can be confusing for visiting Americans. American universities are largely staffed by professors. Most have assistant or associate in their titles to denote lower ranks. Below them are the toiling and untitled instructors. In Britain, people with the title of professor are comparatively rare. It usually distinguishes someone of great achievement in his or her field or an accomplished department chairman. The usual ranks for academics in Britain are, in descending order, *reader, senior lecturer* and *lecturer.* The plain title of *instructor* in Britain usually means someone who teaches in a technical or vocational institution rather than a college or a university. The dilemmas created by having different titles can be circumvented for visiting Americans by simply calling those with the Ph.D. "doctor."

Many Americans expect stereotypical Oxbridge students to appear at all British universities. Instead of undergraduates wearing straw hats and sipping champagne as they discuss Plato, they are apt to encounter a horde of loud, shabbily and drably dressed youngsters who are ferociously committed to party and drink. Some British universities are just as notorious party schools as some American universities in the West which need not be named. Overall, the amount of alcohol and tobacco that British undergraduates consume on the average is simply appalling.

Some Additional Words Needing Translation

Here are some words not fitting into the sections on education above which might be helpful to know:

Campus — is not a word heard in Britain, generally. It is an American import.

Direct Grant School — a private school that receives financial support from the government directly, usually with a provision enabling a number of students from poor families to attend on scholarships.

Form — the noun used to designate "grade" in Britain, as in: "He is in the fifth form."

Headmaster or *Head* — the name of the principal of a British school.

Holidays — vacation periods, for school children and in general.

Maths — Mathematics is always abbreviated in the plural and not in the American singular, "math."

Old Boys and *Old Girls* — the people that Americans speak of as alumni and alumnae.

Polytechnic — an institution that provides some kind of higher education, usually in a technical field, but without university status. Polytechnics do not have resident students ordinarily.

Rag — as in a students' rag, means a time of high spirits and uproariousness, what Americans would call "a time to let off steam."

Send Down — To fail at school for an academic or moral reason results in the student being sent down, or what we would call being kicked out.

"The" as a missing article — British people leave out "the" and "a" or "an" when discussing such institutions as a university. For instance, they are "at university" instead of "at *the* university." The same is true for hospitals. One is "at hospital" in Britain.

RELIGION

Why You Should Go to Church in Britain

Great spires pointing heavenward all over the island attest to Britain's magnificent religious history. But cold statistics demonstrate that most British people do not get near churches or chapels on Sundays. Nominal members, inactive members, agnostics and atheists are found in a greater proportion than in the United

States. The British pattern is similar to the rest of Europe, whereas the United States is noted for a high percentage of the middle class going to church. Even so, devout Britons are not hard to find, and each of the major denominations has a vigorous core operating.

No matter what a visitor's religion or lack of it, going to church in Britain is a valuable cultural experience. The music alone is generally of a high standard. In many churches, a choir of boys provides an angelic sound, most of the time anyway. Great organs are grand in old churches, and congregations have a tendency to sing not only with vigor but with sharp and distinct pronunciation.

Sermons and readings are also in distinct, precise English, although the presentation might be too restrained, orderly, rational and cold for those Americans who are used to loud, emotional sermons on Sunday. But the point is to get out and sample some of what goes on in British churches, where the visitor can feel the past in a real, tangible way. It can be a thrill to be inside a chilly old church or cathedral, hearing an elegant service echoing off ancient stone. Do not pass up such an opportunity.

Sorting Out the Churches: The Established Church

The established church, or official church of the state is the Church of England, also called the C. of E., or the Anglican Church. Since Henry VIII's break with Rome in the early sixteenth century, the Church of England is usually considered a Protestant church. Yet many of its leaders and members today choose to describe it as a catholic church with a small "c." They take the meaning of catholic as "universal," and their church as a church for everyone everywhere. Anglicans describe their church as "apostolic," meaning that they see a direct, unbroken historic line reaching all the way back to the apostles. The Pope's role as leader of the Roman Catholic church is regarded as a late medieval growth of power that was not present in the early church. From their point of view, the Church of England goes all the way back to the time St. Augustine arrived in 597 to convert the heathen Anglo-Saxons.

Outside of England, the church takes on other names. In Wales, it is the Church of Wales and in Ireland the Church of Ireland. By the way, the sparsely attended Church of Ireland's main cathedral in Dublin, St. Patrick's, often confuses tourists who expect it to be Roman Catholic.

The sister church to the Church of England in America is the Episcopal Church. The name, episcopal, simply means having bishops. This name was chosen after the American Revolution because attending the overseas branch of the established church of the recently defeated imperial power was not popular.

Episcopalians are best prepared, of course, to appreciate the Anglican Church. They are familiar with its liturgy, meaning patterns of worship presented in a prayer book. They also accept the emphasis placed upon a version of the Mass called Communion or the Eucharist. Dignity, style and beauty in art and music are features of this denomination.

The Church of England and its sister churches have an informal diversity within. There is a distinction between the so-called "high" churches and the so-called "low" churches. The former put emphasis on historical ceremonies, featuring color, costumes, chants, bells and incense. The latter are much simpler and plainer, stressing the Bible, old English hymns and straightforward sermons. "Broad" churches attempt to incorporate the best of both emphases. Parallels to these high, low and broad styles flourish in the Episcopal Church in the United States, and provide no end of discussion and controversy for Episopalians.

Some explanation of the nature of the sixteenth century Reformation in England is necessary to understand the Anglican Church. It came about suddenly, for almost overnight the Roman Catholic Church became the Anglican Church. The same buildings, the same priests, bishops and archbishops carried on as the Church of England thereafter. There were a few exceptions; some Roman Catholics became martyrs because they were either too principled or too old-fashioned or too rigid, depending upon one's point of view. The most dramatic change from the English Reformation, something that marked the English landscape forever, was the dissolution of the monasteries and convents. Rich church land was sold by the crown to private individuals; monastic buildings were left empty to become ruins, and monks and nuns were pensioned off. The other changes of a Protestant nature were less dramatic, and most of them were introduced gradually, changes such as allowing the marriage of priests, the reduction of the number of sacraments from seven to two (baptism and communion), the end of private confession, the circulation of the Bible in English and greater emphasis upon sermons.

It is hard to define Anglicanism as either Protestant or Catholic. Architecture reflects this problem. On the one hand, the stark and often strikingly beautiful ruins of the monasteries are all over Britain. They were used as quarries for stone and their roofs supplied lead. In their ruined condition, they testify to the force of Henry VIII's Reformation, as well as to the greed of the landowners. But the cathedrals, churches, hospitals, alms houses and other church properties were kept much as they were before the Reformation. Even when the Puritans were active in the seventeenth century, the Anglican artistic heritage was largely saved from their depredations. Therefore, the Church of England does let the visitor sense the long, deep, medieval past of Christianity in Britain.

The Church of Scotland

The Church of Scotland is a Presbyterian Church which has had a very special role in Scottish history. Scots rallied around this church for their early assertions of nationalism. In fact, the civil wars of the seventeenth century were triggered by Scottish resistance to having Anglicanism foisted upon their "kirk," or church.

Today when the British monarch is in Scotland, she attends the Church of Scotland and functions as its leader. American Presbyterians will be interested in contrasting the Church of Scotland practices with their churches at home. They may be left with the conviction that Scottish practices are very "high" compared to American Presbyterian worship, particularly if they attend St. Giles Cathedral in the Royal Mile of Edinburgh. Ironically, St. Giles was the place where violent resistance to Anglicanism first took place. Legend has it that one parishioner, upon hearing of the "Papist" nature of the new Prayer Book imposed by England, flung a stool at the pulpit. Pandemonium followed. Today a bronze plaque marks the spot on the floor where it all began.

Other Protestants: Dissenters and Nonconformists

The Dissenters and Nonconformists are the Protestants who, historically, dissented from the Anglican Church and refused to conform to it. Together, they comprise close to half of all the Protestants in Britain. The Anglicans, if they are called Protestants, make up the other half. In America, Baptists, Presbyterians, Methodists, Quakers and Congregationalists correspond to dissenting Protestants in Britain, with English, but not Scottish, Presbyterians counted as Dissenters. American Congregationalists have a bewildering variety of names besides Congregationalist. In general, they are unattached churches, churches with congregational control and considerable Puritan influence, as their emphasis upon the Bible reveals.

Originally, the Nonconformists began as radical Protestants within the Anglican Church who wished to "purify" it, or make it less like the Roman Catholic Church. They gained the name "Puritans" as a result. In the stress and tumult of the English Civil War, the Puritans broke away into several distinct groups and were no longer contained within the Anglican Church. A century later, in the eighteenth century, the Methodists broke away from the Anglicans. After Puritan leadership in the seventeenth century under Cromwell came to an end, these Protestants were discriminated against in employment, education and in society in general. Nevertheless, their freedom to believe what they wanted, or "liberty of conscience," was tolerated. Despite the flagrant discrimination against them, this limited toleration can be seen as a major step forward in human history. Dissenters who could not hold jobs in government or graduate from Oxford or Cambridge because of their religion could worship in peace in their churches, which were officially called chapels.

Puritans from Britain gave American Protestantism a decided emphasis. All through the seventeenth century, they left England in numbers that were to multiply greatly in the open lands of the New World. The influence of Puritanism has been felt many times in American history, through such movements as temperance, prohibition and laws concerning sexual behavior. The old-fashioned, strict, sober work ethic, so quickly eroding in many places today, can also be attributed to the Puritan heritage.

What about the Puritans who stayed in England? Shut out from politics and many government careers, many Presbyterians, Baptists, Congregationalists and Methodists turned to making money in business. Given their religious discipline that inculcated habits of thrift, industry and sobriety, businessmen from these groups tended to become very prosperous. When the Industrial Revolution began, Dissenters were on hand with substantial capital, business expertise and a willingness to work hard. Many built up tremendous fortunes at the time of industrialization. A number of their richer descendants converted to Anglicanism in order to become part of the establishment, but many remained in old Puritan denominations. The last vestiges of legal discrimination against them were lifted while the Industrial Revolution was in progress.

Visitors should observe how the descendants of the Puritans carry on their worship. Some of their chapels are stark and bare, enabling the worshippers to concentrate on the sermon and Bible readings. Almost everything from the rich medieval traditions of religious symbolism and art is absent. The contrast between a simple Congregationalist chapel and a high Anglican Church should be noted because this contrast reveals the range of Protestantism in England.

Roman Catholicism in Britain

A very substantial minority of the British population adheres to the Roman Catholic Church. Here is another striking similarity with the United States. No other major states of the Western world have a Protestant majority and a Roman Catholic minority in these proportions. Germany once did, but the division of Germany after World War II left West Germany with a roughly even split between Protestants and Catholics. The other countries in the world having Protestant majorities have small populations, Sweden or Australia, for example.

Roman Catholics in Britain today come from two historical streams. "Old" English Catholics are those who resisted the Reformation and preserved the faith even in those desperate days when Henry VIII, Elizabeth I and Oliver Cromwell hounded their priests. Old English Catholics have traditions of private masses held in secret, of priests hidden away in unlikely places and of unflinching resistance to attempts to convert them to Protestantism. Many of these old English Catholics were in prominent families living in conservative rural areas far from London.

The other stream of Roman Catholics emanated from Ireland, particularly after the British Industrial Revolution created a great demand for unskilled labor. The major industrial cities of Britain today, including Liverpool, Manchester, Glasgow and London, have substantial populations of Irish ancestry. In the nineteenth century, the Irish came to work as "navvies," construction workers on the railroads, or as factory hands. They took jobs as Mexicans take many jobs in the United States today, accepting low pay for doing something that the native-born shun. Emigration to Britain and America became a flood as a result of the dreadful Irish potato famine at mid-century. In the twentieth century, drift out of Ireland to jobs in Britain has continued, but on a much smaller scale.

The rough proletarian Roman Catholics who came to Britain from Ireland turned out to be much stauncher Catholics in their adopted country than they had been at home, and the same can be said for Irish Catholics in America. The Roman Catholic Church became a means to preserve their identity and culture in their new Protestant environments.

Jews in Britain

Like the United States, Britain has long had a reputation as being a good environment for Jews. As a result, substantial numbers of people of the Jewish faith comprise an important if small component of the populations of both countries. This reputation does not go all the way back in England, because there were brutal medieval persecutions. Perhaps the most famous of them occurred at Clifford's Tower in York, where Jews threatened and surrounded chose mass suicide. For a long time, Jews were officially banned from England, although many continued to live in the country surreptitiously. Jews were welcomed back to England in the seventeenth century by Oliver Cromwell and the Puritans who, ironically, were noted for persecuting Roman Catholics. Puritans appreciated Jews because they were living witnesses to the Old Testament. Others did not, and Jew baiting continued into the nineteenth century.

Over the centuries, groups of Jews came to Britain to escape the pogroms, persecutions and ghettos of Continental Europe. The last great influx was in the era of World War II, when refugees from Nazi persecution followed the old emigration routes. Here again Britain and the United States share an aspect of history.

There is a sweeping generalization about the assimilation of Jews in Western society that makes sense geographically: the further east one goes in Europe, the less the assimilation; the further west, the greater the assimilation. Most Jews in Poland and Russia would be locked in their own communities, either in separate Jewish small towns or in ghettos or districts in the cities. In Germany, farther west, Jews would undergo more assimilation, experiencing the cultural stress of becoming less distinctly Jewish and more German. In Britain, the furthest western country in Europe, Jews became the most assimilated, and very British.

This is not to say that anti-semitism has been absent from Britain in recent times. Those who saw the film "Chariots of Fire" were exposed to the rather subtle anti-semitism of gentlemen in the early twentieth century. Benjamin Disraeli, who was Prime Minister in the latter nineteenth century, and the converted son of a Jewish man of letters, had to endure more blatant anti-semitism. When he rose in the House of Commons to give his first speech, members drowned out his voice with shouts of "Old Clothes!" a reference to a trade that many Jewish immigrants made their specialty when they came to Britain.

Today a much more subtle and low key anti-semitism still exists, and it is probably connected to the high degree of class consciousness in Britain. But over against this is an enduring tradition of British liberalism and commitment to democracy that despises anti-semitism in any form.

CLASS AND SEX IN BRITAIN

Class Consciousness

Feelings about class in Britain are pervasive, insidious and frequently charged with emotion. The United States does not have class feelings on anything approaching this scale, unless subtle or blatant racial feelings, all too pervasive even today, are used as the basis for comparison with the strains and tensions of class feelings in Britain.

Class discrimination might comprise the very worst feature of life in Britain. American visitors will not encounter any class-conscious expressions directed at them because Americans stand outside the British class system. In fact, class antagonisms are often flashed in such a subtle way that visitors might miss the inferences entirely.

Why do these class antagonisms exist? Various explanations have been offered. One argument sees class antagonisms going all the way back in history to the time that the upper landed classes imposed their dominance, first by force and then through heredity and wealth. Since Britain never experienced a French-style revolution, in which the lower orders rose to topple the upper class, the dominance of the upper class was never broken in Britain and continues on today.

An explanation favored by the ultra-conservatives is that the most able people established their ascendancy by the laws of survival of the fittest long ago, and just as fast horses breed fast horses, able people have produced long lines of talented individuals. Therefore, it is argued, people in the lower classes are generally less able human beings of lower intelligence. Some go so far as to imply that those at the bottom have interests and activities that are much more animalistic than those of the people at the top. The argument goes on to declare that the people at the commanding heights of society have always been charged with the responsibility of maintaining civilization in the face of lower class barbarism. Therefore, they deserve their privileges.

Another argument used to explain class in Britain is that human groups have always antagonistically disputed sharing the earth's riches. Since England has always had relatively few people of other ethnic stocks or skin colors, white Anglo-Saxon Protestants have divided themselves into classes in order to exercise rivalry and conflict. This view sees group antagonisms as natural to the species everywhere. Therefore, what could be more natural than two similar American communities close to each other on the plains of North Dakota convinced that the members of the respective opposite basketball team are worthy objects of hatred?

Still another explanation, popular among Marxists, relates class differences to the economy. Since the means of production are owned by one group and the work is done by another group, classes must exist, and where there are classes there are class struggles.

No matter which of these arguments or what combination of arguments is used to explain class antagonisms in Britain, nobody will deny their existence. A definition of class divisions is needed, but the dynamic changes of modern society make defining difficult.

An Attempt at Defining Classes in Britain

In the past, a fairly clear division into three classes could be perceived in Britain: upper, middle and lower, or, using alternative terms, the aristocratic (or landed) class, the bourgeoisie and the working class, which can also be called the proletariat. To simplify things, most people could be placed in one of these three categories by determining how they received their money. Those who lived off rents and payments on property that they owned, especially inherited land, were upper class. Those who shuffled pieces of paper around for a living, either in business or in one of the professions, were bourgeois or middle class. This class had a broad range, from high income bankers to low income shopkeepers and clerks. Those who actually touched work materials were working class or proletarian. For instance, the carpenter touched wood, the butcher touched meat and the plumber touched pipes.

In recent times, class definitions have been blurred. This has largely been attributable to the creation of so many semi-professional and technical jobs that may or may not be considered middle class. Some new definitions of working class have been tried out, but difficulties have arisen in applying them. Take, for example, the current definition of a working class job as one that the worker regards as repetitive, unchallenging and as likely to be carried out in generally unpleasant surroundings.

No matter how difficult it is to come up with definitions that fit a host of anomalies, there is a broad gulf in Britain between what is considered middle class and what is called working class. The gulf is confirmed by dozens of subtle and blatant indicators, revealing an individual as either "one of them" or "one of us."

Speech is the most ready indicator of class. In most cases, pronunciation gives class identity away before the first sentence is finished. There are only two ways to speak in England (but not in Scotland or Wales): properly or improperly. To maintain their children's proper speech, the middle and upper classes gladly spend their money on tuition at the "right" schools so that class and regional afflictions of speech will not contaminate them. Accent is one thing; choice of words is another. People on one side of the great gulf of class will say such things as "the missus," instead of "my wife," which is intoned by people on the other side. Hundreds of words used by lower class speakers are never used by those who speak proper English, and vice versa. Over time, a rich slang has developed in working class life, creating nicknames and abbreviations for all sorts of objects and situations. But should any of these slang terms be used accidentally in a setting where only proper English is acceptable, it can be construed as an embarrassing gaffe.

Other indicators of class abound, including the way people dress; the magazines and newspapers they read; how and where they spend their leisure time; what clubs they belong to; where they live; whether or not they own their own domicile; where they went to school; where they vacation; what cars they drive; whether or not they have a car; and what TV programs they enjoy.

Two British TV comedy programs occasionally shown in the United States reveal something about class in Britain. Those who watch "Monty Python's Flying Circus" in Britain probably avoid the "Benny Hill Show." On the other hand, it has to be admitted that the effect of television has apparently lessened some of the differences between classes in Britain. Before World War II, George Orwell could single out certain striking behaviors of the working class, such as comfortably wearing hats indoors, taking cheese from the point of a knife and drinking tea from the saucer. Since TV, it may be hard to find working class persons who do these without self-consciousness.

While class differences remain a constant source of humor in Britain, there are serious effects as a result of class distinctions that are not at all beneficial. Because of class, sniggering contempt, hostility, rancor, jealousy and, at worst, outright hatred can flare, particularly when an event such as a strike brings class consciousness to the fore. At such a time, each side looking across the gulf of class seems to see a stereotype. To the employer and managerial classes, the working classes can appear particularly lazy, mean, gross, dirty, insensitive, unpatriotic, stupid and narrow-minded. Conversely, workers see the employers as stupid and narrow-minded, as well as spoiled, lucky, selfish, greedy, false, artificial and, at worst, truly vicious. Another stereotype held by each of the classes is a favorable self-image. Workers regard themselves as the "real" people of the nation, the salt of the earth who do not put on airs. They are the people who do the essential hard work that actually keeps the nation going. Their demands, from this point of view, are only for a fair share of what they create through working. The middle and upper classes, on the other hand, see themselves as almost sole possessors of brains maintaining the dynamism and decency of the nation, without whom the working classes would be hopeless slugs.

Bitterness over the gulf of class is unfortunately deep and enduring in Britain. It can flare up in all sorts of places in addition to the workplace. It can

come between doctor and patient, librarian and
reader, householder and maintenance man, and
ticket-taker and passenger.

Americans and Class

Americans in Britain are often taken by surprise
when such class feelings arise. Sometimes they are confused by tales of malicious behavior that one class casts
upon another in a "them" versus "us" setting. As has
been mentioned, racial hostility in American history
can be compared in some ways to British class enmity,
as can some ethnic divisions in American history.
Nevertheless, the class consciousness of an ordinary
American is generally blurred and undeveloped by
comparison to his British counterpart for several good
reasons.

America has always been a more open, more ex-
pansive, less traditional society. In spreading itself
across a continent rapidly, the United States has come
to incorporate diverse regions and diverse lifestyles. As
a consequence, preoccupation with various indicators
of class does not play a part in American life as it does
in Britain. Take accents, for an example. In recent
decades, President Kennedy had a New England
twang, President Johnson had a Texas drawl, and
President Carter a southern accent. While media announcers stress the bland sound of the Midwest,
Americans are unlikely to be prejudiced simply by the
way people talk.

Americans tend to have masses of people rather
than classes of people. Sociologists in the United States
constantly refine and redraw the tests used in the difficult task of putting people in class categories. Ask
Americans what class they belong to and nearly all of

them will respond "middle class," no matter if they are highly affluent professionals or service workers paid close to the minimum wage and living in very modest surroundings. Declaring that one is middle class in America seems to involve maintaining a belief in the American dream of living well, either at present or in the future. For most people, being middle class does not necessarily mean, as it would in Britain, achieving a certain level of education, maintaining certain forms of social behavior or holding particular jobs. Many Europeans have great difficulty understanding class in America.

This is not to deny that some broad divisions do exist in American society. For instance, there is a division between college educated and non-college educated. Even so, countless people take courses as adults and many get degrees late in life. There is also a division between blue collar and white collar workers, but countless jobs fall between these classifications. While doctors, lawyers and architects obviously belong to high paying and high prestige professions, in America a high percentage of them undoubtedly served in restaurants, held down repetitive factory types of jobs or worked at some other low paying, low prestige jobs. It is much harder for a young person of high ambition and talents to take up a menial job in Britain and then get out of that menial job. On the other hand, Americans know that the young person handing out baskets of fried chicken can be a senator some day. Americans are not "pegged" by what they do for a living during one period of their lives, and this is one of the great boons from living in this country.

In newer parts of the United States, but to a degree in all parts, the dominant determinant of class is money instead of education, taste, behavior of various kinds or language. If one has large amounts of money, one is considered upper class, and if one has little, one is lower class. Those with some make up the great mass in the middle. From a sociologist's standpoint, this is a glaring, sweeping oversimplification. To the ordinary American, it most often seems like the truth.

Of Men and Women

It is very difficult to generalize about the respective roles of men and women in Britain and the United States at this stage in history because there are all kinds of men and all kinds of women in any community, and they form all kinds of relationships. Undoubtedly, a highly significant and inexorable revolution in the relations of men and women and, consequently, in the structure of the family, has been going on in the Western world. This vast social revolution is far from over, and since we are all caught up in it somehow, an understanding of its significance, implications and ultimate results is far from clear, whether we live in Britain or in the United States. What is clear is that it is a much debated and discussed matter, with emotions, interest and controversies operating at high levels.

It appears that this formidable revolution has proceeded at a faster pace and has gone the furthest in the United States. Equal opportunities on a broad social and legal front have been achieved to a greater degree in the United States than in Britain. This is not to deny the successes gained by a long tradition of ardent feminism in Britain, highlighted by the celebrated suffragettes of the Edwardian era who championed women's right to vote. Recently, feminist groups on British campuses have taken notable *avant garde* positions. Yet when the various activities of feminist and women's groups in Britain are taken into consideration, it appears that many of them are relatively isolated in positions far in advance of the mainstream of British women. Comparable American groups, it can be argued, are not as far out front in advance of ordinary American women.

Translated into ordinary circumstances, this means that most British women continue to act in traditional ways. They will be more apt to defer to masculine judgment, wit, knowledge, strength and understanding, as their mothers were purported to do. At the same time, they will seek to maintain a mysteriousness about their intuition, charm and spiritual powers. They will expect deferential treatment from men at the same time that they will try to be highly manipulative of the men who are openly acknowledged to be so wise and so strong. In other words, the male and female roles prevailing in the 1950s and in all of the previous centuries are far from over in Britain for millions of people. American visitors accustomed to the new relationships in the United States might be taken aback by this. Americans of a more traditional caste might feel more comfortable in Britain with this aspect of life.

There is an irony here. No matter how far behind the British drive towards equal rights may appear in comparison to developments in the United States, women in Britain have long been regarded as far in advance of the rest of the world. Even as far back as the sixteenth century the independence, assertiveness and freedom of English women was mentioned frequently by foreign visitors. Of course, these views were offered by males who securely dominated society. In that century, Elizabeth I enhanced appreciation of women's abilities, although she, too, played the game of feminine deference when it suited her purposes. In subsequent centuries, intellectual females in Britain gained worldwide renown in philosophy and literature. They included Mary Wollstonecroft, the Brontë sisters, and George Eliot, who took that pseudonym in deference to male chauvinism. These women and the militant suffragettes who followed them had to fight an uphill battle against the slowly crumbling bastions of male power and even more slowly crumbling resistance of male prejudice.

The struggle for sexual equality is far from over, and even if Mrs. Thatcher is Prime Minister, women in America remain ahead of women in Britain on this score. Certainly Mrs. Thatcher has frequently demonstrated her ability and authority, regardless of what one thinks of her political stance, and this should have a significantly beneficial effect on the campaign for equal rights. The direction does seem to be set towards greater and greater female participation in all of life's activities and tasks, with equal compensation for equal effort. In this, as in so much else in the twentieth century, Britain seems to be following rather than leading developments taking place in the United States.

One particular aspect of male/female relationships that should be mentioned before ending this section is the particularly British phenomenon of "chatting up." Naturally, males talk to females to impress them, and vice versa, everywhere, and no matter whether the games of the 1980s or the 1950s or 1050s are being played. What makes this a remarkably British pastime is the intensity of the phenomenon. Flirtation with words is something carried on everywhere by people of all ages. Word games become very elaborate and are characterized by flashes of humor and cleverness. Here is yet another example of the great importance of language in this country. Rumor does have it, though, that when relations proceed far beyond chatting, Britons are apt to display an intensity that is both very serious and very quiet!

CHAPTER FOUR

Understanding British Politics

WHY MOST AMERICANS ARE DISCONCERTED WHEN THEY DISCUSS POLITICS IN BRITAIN

Once in Britain, Americans quickly learn that comparable British people know much more about politics than they do. It becomes obvious that they know far more about American politics than the visiting Americans know about British politics. It does not stop there. Britons seem to know much more about the political affairs of the whole world. Perhaps they are so keen on politics because of the long tradition of successful political developments in Britain. Perhaps it is because they were at the center of a worldwide empire for so long, or perhaps it is because they have been, in recent decades, a small state highly dependent upon developments in foreign places. The pervasive influence of the serious British Broadcasting Corporation newscasts is undoubtedly a contributing factor. So is the penchant of most British people to read a great deal in newspapers, magazines and books.

The upshot is that Britons will invariably have many clever and insightful things to say about American political leaders and situations. Ordinary Britons will have some sharp remark about whoever is President and over whatever subject is at the forefront of news in America. Despite the Briton's sharpness, there are some areas murky to him or her, particularly regionalism and the role of the states. The British emphasis in discussing American politics tends to focus on personalities who are well known throughout the world.

The American visitor is not likely to have similar comments to make about British politics or politicians. While he or she might know something about remarkable Margaret Thatcher, and have a glowing memory of Winston Churchill as a great hero, all of the other British politicians — Wilson, Heath, Foot, Callaghan and many more — are blurred. The American cannot say much about them the way the Briton can speak about Reagan, Carter, Ford, Nixon and Johnson. Even worse, the British Parliamentary system is probably a mystery. Since ignorance about how the British system works might reflect on the visitor's political knowledge, the following sections are included to cast light on the subject.

UNDERSTANDING THE BRITISH PARLIAMENTARY SYSTEM

Basic Differences from the American System

The British parliamentary system has been a celebrated success for a long time at home and in the vigorous "daughter" nations, Canada, New Zealand and Australia. This goes a long way in explaining why nearly all the new representative governments that have come into existence in recent decades have adopted one variation or another of the British parliamentary system. Almost no nations have sought to adopt the American system with a presidential executive, Congress as the legislature and the courts functioning as a judicial branch. All of these branches are supposed to operate under the sacred principles of the separation of powers and the application of checks and balances.

High school American social studies or civics classes that extol the virtues of our Constitution would be uncomfortable making a comparative study of the British parliamentary system. Why? Because Britain is a free country without checks and balances, without separation of powers, without federalism and without a written constitution.

All actual power resides in the House of Commons. So, in effect, the British system is unicameral, having only one chamber that really counts. The all-powerful executive is the Cabinet, otherwise known as the Government, and the Prime Minister presides over it. The Prime Minister is at the same time the leader of the party in the House of Commons that has a majority in that body.

What a contrast this makes to the American system! Our cabinet members are required not to hold seats in the Congress in order to ensure the separation of powers. British Cabinet members almost invariably must be strong leaders in the House of Commons.

Other Differences: The Constitution

British people never have to worry about whether a proposed piece of legislation is constitutional or unconstitutional. If it passes into law in the House of Commons, it becomes part of the Constitution immediately. All of the laws on the books, called statutes, make up the British Constitution. There are also some hoary documents which we as Americans are entitled to share, namely, Magna Carta of 1215, the Petition of Right of 1628 and the Bill of Rights of 1689.

Despite the existence of these documents and all of the unrepealed statutes, the British Constitution is declared to be "unwritten." Indeed, part of the Constitution involves operating on long-entrenched customs and precedents, much in the same way that the United States Constitution does not specify how the political parties operate to produce candidates. Nowhere does one read about national party conventions in our Constitution.

Since the British Constitution can be changed by the vote of a simple majority in the House of Commons, the British Constitution can be extremely flexible and responsive to new needs. By contrast, an elaborate procedure must be followed to change the American Constitution, or the Supreme Court must interpret aspects of it at the end of an elaborate judicial process. The long struggle for the Equal Rights Amendment is an apt example of something that would not have to happen in Britain.

Other Differences: Political Style

Interruptions, heckling, shouts and even tumult often break out in the House, usually in the middle of somebody's attempt to make a speech. It is not the usual style for the better politicians in the United States, but rough-and-tumble at the top has been the style in Britain for a long time.

The same style operates in local campaigns, especially when candidates "stand" — not "run" — for office and show up at "the hustings," or election meetings. ("Hustings" is always used in the plural, by the way.) Candidates must stand on their own two feet and fend off the attacks that come from random constituents on the floor. Sometimes these attacks take the form of crude interruptions and nasty heckling, and the only way to face up to them is head on. With skill, the audience can be turned on the heckler in derision, but it is always up to the candidate to defend himself or herself. Here is another example of how highly regarded verbal skills are in that nation.

Other Differences: When a Government Fails

Ordinarily presidents cannot be dislodged for four years, senators for six years and members of the House of Representatives for two years. British members of Parliament, or M.P.s, as they are invariably known, can be dislodged and the whole government can come tumbling down any day.

The Prime Minister, known as the P.M., has what baseball fans would call a fielder's choice. The P.M. can either serve out a full five-year term and then hold elections, or the P.M. can call for elections at any time. Theoretically, any Prime Minister and his or her

Cabinet can also be overthrown by an adverse vote on a major piece of legislation on the floor of the House of Commons. But party discipline prevents this situation from developing as it did in the last century, when Prime Ministers were expected to resign under such circumstances. Party discipline imposes upon members of the majority party the imperative to vote with the Prime Minister and the Cabinet. Disloyalty can be severely punished at the next election time. Even so, a scandal as grave as Watergate would have toppled a British Prime Minister more quickly than when Nixon was ousted because such an issue would bring M.P.s to vote on the basis of conscience alone.

So today it is really a question of taking the full five years or calling for fresh elections before that period is up. Prime Ministers usually wait for a time when a tide of public support seems to be running in their favor before calling for an election. The aim is to add to the majority already existing and to prolong the length of time that the party controls the government.

Sometimes Prime Ministers miscalculate in calling an "early" election — early meaning before the term is up — and find themselves out of office because a majority of the opposition party members of Parliament have been elected. Then, too, some governments last the whole five years without ever perceiving the tide running strongly for them and decide to fight it out at the end of the term instead. Regardless of what option the Prime Minster takes, the unpredictability of election contests adds a note of excitement to British politics absent from our own.

The formalities observed in calling an election are colorful. The Prime Minister must seek out the queen and ask that the sovereign grant a dissolution of Parliament. It is theoretically the queen's Parliament and the queen's Cabinet and the queen's Prime Minister, and she can call Parliament into session or dismiss it at will. In actuality, she dutifully does what the politicians tell her to do.

When Parliament is dissolved, all the members run for office in their individual constituencies. After the returns are in, the leader of the party with a majority in the House of Commons is summoned by the queen and asked to form a government. This means that the victor can pick a cabinet and serve as Prime Minister. Of course, the queen will summon whoever has the backing of a majority in the House of Commons. She has no real choice because she is a constitutional sovereign who must act as a ceremonial figurehead only. Long ago, the choice of ministers was the sovereign's alone, as the ritual ceremony testifies.

Other Differences: The Loyal Opposition

The Prime Minister and other Cabinet members sit on one of the two "front benches" of the House of Commons, either the one to the left or the one to the right of the impartial Speaker who presides. People of lesser importance sit farther back, and are called "backbenchers," which is another word for "rank and file." The people who occupy the other "front bench" in the House of Commons, shortened in most uses simply to "House," are the leaders of the opposition. They form a "shadow cabinet," a group of leaders ready to form a government when their opponents lose an election and become a minority instead of a majority. Until that happens, they sit right across the way, a few feet from their opponents' "front bench" and at eye level with them. During debate and questioning periods, the opposition is capable of mounting direct attacks on the Prime Minister and the other ministers unlike anything that the American President or cabinet members have to face. The closest our leaders come to it is during heated news conferences.

The adjective "loyal" has some historical significance. Once it was thought that those who opposed the monarch's ministers opposed the monarch. This was often the case, certainly, but as the monarchs were increasingly removed from the fulcrum of political power, the concept that politicians could oppose the monarch's ministers and still be loyal to the crown and state began to be accepted. They could oppose and yet be loyal. How many governments are there in the world today which cannot tolerate any opposition, where those who oppose are automatically regarded as opponents? The concept of a "loyal opposition," first developed in Britain, is essential for true political freedom to flourish.

Other Differences: Efficiency in Government

The British are freed from the elaborate procedures required to keep the American presidency, Senate and House of Representatives functioning together. All of the negotiating, arm-twisting, threats and compromises between these bodies are not needed in Britain because everything emanates from the House of Commons where all of the real power resides. It is the only organ of the central government in which all the elected members sit together, the ministers and their opponents. This brings a speed and an efficiency in government that the American system simply cannot muster, except in a time of dire emergency. Political maneuvering certainly preoccupies

British politicians also, but it usually goes on within the respective parties, rather than between organs of government.

Other Differences: Efficient Elections

No subject more clearly reveals the efficiency of the British system in comparison to ours than the nature of elections. Our campaigns seem to stretch on endlessly. For example, our presidential contests get underway years in advance of the actual election date. Since congressmen must stand for reelection every two years and senators every six, and since each state has a governor and a legislature that also seeks reelection, the American scene is one of almost constant electioneering. Campaigns never seem to end, so there never seems to be any freedom from all of their fundraisers, sloganeering and hoopla.

By contrast, British campaigns are short and inexpensive. Why? One reason is that a whole layer of election activity does not exist because the federal system does not exist. More important is the fact that the time for campaigning is strictly demarcated as a period of a few weeks. The amount of money that can be spent by each candidate is also limited.

Another Difference: The Tone of Elections

Individual candidates on each side of the Atlantic will provide sharp contrasts to the generalization that the tone of British election campaigns is pitched higher. Moreover, it cannot be denied that repetitious slogans, slick TV ads and glib half-truths are used in Britain as well as here. Nevertheless, there does seem to be much more emphasis on debate and intelligent arguments. British candidates seem to aim more at the voters' minds and common sense than at their apprehensions, fears and greed.

UNDERSTANDING THE HOUSE OF LORDS

Americans in Britain who discuss politics are likely to be teased about the U.S. Senate. No matter how populous or how empty, each state produces two senators. How can this be in a democracy? How can Nevada have the same representation as California?

Strangely enough, the U.S. Senate is based upon the British upper house, the House of Lords. The Duke of this or the Earl of that or the Baron of the other were all territorially based, often having a shire as their name. Together, the British House of Lords represented vast sections of the British countryside. The Senate represents territories also, the states.

An obvious major difference between senators and members of the House of Lords is that the former are elected and most of the latter inherit their positions. The first-born son inherits the title and the seat upon the death of his father. His siblings are in law non-noble, although they sometimes have courtesy titles. Since 1958, "life peers" have been selected to recognize the achievements of distinguished individuals. They cannot pass on their titles. In addition, women have taken seats in the House of Lords in recent years.

Everyone in this aristocratic house is supposed to be in a special noble caste, but they are supposed to be peers, meaning equals, to each other. The term "peer" is preferred to lord, which is only used as part of a specific name.

All of the members of the House of Lords either had ancestors appointed to that body by a monarch or were appointed themselves. Distinguished persons would receive an elaborate declaration called a letter patent, ennobling him and, until recent years, his first-born male heirs. Historically, only great landholders in the realm who had rendered outstanding service to the crown, usually through holding important offices or providing wartime leadership, were recipients of letters patent. For similar service, lesser folk might gain a knighthood, a non-noble title in Britain.

In recent centuries, patronage over appointing peers has been taken over by the leading politicians, along with nearly all of the other honors that the crown can dispense. Political contributions have been paid off with titles and seats in the House of Lords, a practice that has drawn criticism for debasing the upper house. The charge has been made that politicians such as David Lloyd George sold seats. Furthermore, those becoming peers were no longer from established, landed families. Many were from business. In fact, the peerage was once called "the beerage" after a number of beer manufacturers who were heavy political contributors gained the scarlet and ermine robes, the uniform for the House of Lords.

While the U.S. Senate is still as powerful as ever, the British House of Lords has been deprived of nearly every bit of power. Powerlessness was arrived at early in this century, as a result of some very complex political history. Since then, all that the House of Lords can do is delay legislation briefly, talk and fulfill colorful ceremonial purposes.

Much of what the peers do talk about informally concerns medicine and doctors, because a good many of them are very old men. Even so, the formal debates in the House of Lords are often quite worth while, since the members are entirely independent of the electorate and incapable of influencing the House of Commons in any way except by persuasion.

Politicians on the extreme left call for the abolition of the House of Lords, declaring it to be a useless and expensive anachronism. For most British people, however, it is like the crown in being one of those priceless links with the past, present and future.

UNDERSTANDING THE BRITISH MONARCHY

Why Americans Are Closet Royalists

Like the House of Lords, the monarchy exists in the modern world in order to carry on ceremonial functions. Although powerless in politics, the monarchy is the greatest of all the ancient institutions linking the generations of the past, the present and the future. Somewhat surprisingly, it also links countless members of the democratic republic across the Atlantic with the royal past. Americans have always been fascinated by the kings and queens of Britain, as demonstrated by the enthusiasm brought forth by every royal visit to the United States. No place outside of the Commonwealth is more willing to go all out celebrating a royal arrival. Moreover, popular magazines in America dwell on the lives of the members of the royal family almost as much as some popular magazines and newspapers in Britain. Indeed, the wit who described Americans as closet royalists was probably correct.

How can this be in a nation that has always appeared to be so staunchly small "r" republican? Perhaps because the British monarchy is a link with our own historic past, a past often thin and barely recognizable in the newer America of rootless, wheeled suburbia. Queen Elizabeth I, Henry VIII, Henry V, Richard the Lionhearted and even King Arthur were monarchs of all the English-speaking people, and so until 1776 they were also the monarchs of the ancestors of what has become the dominant American ethnic component. After all, the British flag flew over the American frontier for 169 years, from Jamestown to 1776. In short, Americans have put in their claim on a long stretch of the history of the British monarchy.

There is something more. Why do housewives in Cheyenne, Wyoming, keep up with the royal behavior of Prince Charles and Princess Diana, more than 200 years after British sovereigns ceased to be American sovereigns? Shouldn't this go against the grain in the American republic, considering its heroic images of self-made men and women and the vigorous, emphatic denial of inherited class distinctions all through its history? Perhaps the answer lies in the realm of fantasy, glamour and magic. Perhaps the repression of feelings or romance about monarchy in our uncompromising republicanism leads to a heightened preoccupation with the British monarchy by certain Americans. Childhood stories about princes and princesses may have much to do with the phenomenon also.

Regardless of the exact psychological origin, it is undeniable that the British monarchy is one of the great lures for American tourists. For their part, the British are brilliantly adept at heightening and perpetuating the drama surrounding the throne. As one young Briton explained to visiting Americans, the crown is "Show Biz" today. Yet it has been show business since it started, since the first Anglo-Saxon monarchs put on their shinier and fancier armor. It will remain one of the most magnificent shows on earth so long as Britain remains a kingdom, a situation which looks as if it will continue forever. After all, could the bands play and the red-coated soldiers march to change the guard at Buckingham Palace if there were no monarchy?

The Value of the Monarchy to Britain

The monarchy is simply wonderful for tourism. Despite the criticisms against it from the far left over the expense of whopping salaries paid to individual members of the royal family, the royal establishment undoubtedly pays for itself many times over through the lure for tourism that royalty's color, traditions and enhancement of history provide.

There are other payoffs for British subjects, who never have more than a small minority of republicans among them. No matter what shocking changes might happen, such as unilateral disarmament, a thoroughgoing socialist regime or the collapse of the pound, there will always be an England, and the monarchy is an indissoluble link in this continuity.

Another psychological consolation from the monarchy is the binding of the generation of today to all the generations of the past by this living institution. Parents of toddlers can anticipate their offspring being ruled by a contemporary royal toddler someday. In an era of adverse effects from what has been called "future shock," inability to adjust to a plethora of changes that come along too fast, there is undoubtedly

a very beneficial psychological payoff for British subjects in having a strong bond of almost predictable
continuity through the crown.

Royal Ribbon-Cutting

Another benefit of the monarchy to Britain is that
there is always someone of dignity and importance to
cut ribbons, launch ships, lay cornerstones, pass out
awards, make dedications and show up at ground-
breaking and various other kinds of important
ceremonies. Such activity is one of the most important
functions of most of the members of the British royal
family, and they do these things with style. Meanwhile,
the Prime Minister and other members of the Cabinet
are free to carry on with their important work.

By contrast, our harried presidents must steal time
from the vital affairs of state so that they can nip out
into the Rose Garden for a ceremony. Often the First
Lady must leave the White House and her husband in
order to fly somewhere for a ribbon-cutting or dedication. The vice-president can be sent, of course, but
most vice-presidents come across flat or colorless when
contrasted to the aura that a president or a prince can
lend to an occasion. Even the Boy Scouts can be let
down when the vice-president substitutes for the chief
of state.

Other democracies that do not have a crowned
Head of State, West Germany for example, have a
high ceremonial office above the real power center.
The Chancellor exercises day-to-day political power,
but the President of the Federal Republic, ceremonial-
ly above him, will have the stature to take the load of
glory off the Chancellor's back, much in the same way
that the British royal family frees up the time of the

Prime Minister.

The Royal Family as a Sponge for the Media

Another benefit of the monarchy accrues to the hardworking politicians in the Cabinet. Since the tabloids and gossip mills go overboard in relating the real and imagined activities of the members of the royal family, Cabinet members are more free from media interference. Leading politicians, their wives and children are all shielded to an extent from the glare and the annoyance of excessive journalistic zeal by the royal family acting as a sponge for this attention.

In the United States there is no such sponge. In recent decades, the First Family in the White House has had to deal with pressure from journalists that has been reminiscent of that put upon Britain's royalty.

The Royal Family as a Model of Deportment

Still another benefit of the monarchy, at least since the times of Queen Victoria, 1837 to 1901, has been the display of a standard of behavior, dress and propriety to guide subjects who wish to appear correct but are unsure of themselves. This is why the social behavior, general deportment and even the clothes of the entire royal family, from the queen downwards, are subject to such intense observation.

For some Britons, especially those who are on the left, ranging from sophisticated intellectuals to poor workers, it all appears to be a stuffy, expensive, showy and even dull extravaganza at taxpayers' expense. But for upper middle-class types and would-be upper middle-class types throughout the world, the royal family provides cues and models for their activities.

Since the times of Queen Victoria, a high standard of proper behavior has been expected from the members of the royal family. All of the celebrated virtues of the wellborn and well raised are supposed to find their noblest expression in the palace. Indeed, if the hallmark of a British lady or gentleman is in making other people feel at ease, certain members of the royal family are masters of the art. They have style, magnificent style, and no matter how staunchly republican a visitor to the palace might be, he or she is more than likely to leave with a keen appreciation of royal grace in action.

Royal Scandals

Under all of their trappings, individual members of the royal family are only human beings, and it is not surprising that the strict standards of behavior expected of them have not always been maintained. This has been particularly observed in the troubled area of sexual expression.

To be sure, many royal figures of old were quite debauched, including Victoria's wicked old uncles. Victoria herself made a mark on social history by trying throughout her reign to set a standard for sexual propriety, a standard much admired by the middle classes. Even though it often drew ribald humor from some aristocrats on one end of the scale and from many British workers on the other, the middle-class standard dominated the nineteenth century, declaring that all sexual activity be confined to marriage alone.

Ever since it was established, the Victorian standard for sexual propriety has been violated by royal scandals. Her own son, Edward VII, was an adulterer, and the next Edward, Edward VIII, became the Duke of Windsor when he abdicated after his romance and marriage to a twice-divorced American woman, Wallis Simpson. Princess Margaret, sister to the present queen, suffered from marriage and divorce problems. The courtship activities of Prince Charles raised many eyebrows, and most recently the activities of Prince Andrew with an American actress gained him the sobriquet "Randy Andy."

Journalists' pursuit of royal sexual peccadilloes borders upon insensitivity and, of course, goes far over the line of common decency and good taste. Dealing with harassment of this sort is one of the more unfortunate aspects of the job of being royal.

The Unreality of Royal Power

Scholars of the medieval period have long carried on spirited debates over how powerful the British monarchy was at this or that period of history. There is no debate about royal power today: The real power of the crown has dried up.

In theory, the queen has all kinds of power, but these powers are entirely imaginary. For instance, only the queen can call Parliament and dismiss Parliament, acts that can be carried out whenever she wishes. She can appoint anybody to any post, from the Prime Minister to an admiral to office clerk. She can also veto any and all legislation to come from the House of Commons and the House of Lords, and do so absolutely. This, by the way, was the origin of the American presidential veto. No monarch has ever tried to veto any bill since the early eighteenth century.

As head of the the Church of England, she can appoint and dismiss all archbishops, bishops, deans and priests. As the fountainhead of all honors, she can theoretically create new peers, hand out memberships in chivalric orders, such as the Order of the Garter, create knights and dispense various other distinctions.

What sometimes mystifies American tourists is that the monarch seems to be carrying out at least some of these powers. Nevertheless, it is all show. Her power is hollow, and what she does is carefully orchestrated by the duly-elected government. She passes out the honors they tell her to pass out; she appoints and dismisses whomever they tell her to appoint or dismiss; she calls and dissolves Parliament when they tell her to do it.

These are the functions of the constitutional monarchy as it has evolved to the present day and, should any ruler be so silly as to try to transmute imaginary power to real power, a resolution would probably be passed in the House of Commons declaring that the monarch has abdicated and wishing a long life to the new monarch, the heir. Since all know the rules, they all perform the way they should.

The monarch's imaginary power is displayed whenever the queen dutifully reads her speech from the throne to her assembled Parliament. Her words are literally chosen by the Prime Minister of the day, so that under one government Her Majesty will make a Conservative speech and under another she will make a speech for the Labour Party. The sovereign simply says what the politicians in power request her to say.

The ancient ceremony of opening Parliament is perhaps the most magnificent display of imaginary power. The bejeweled and dazzling monarch sits in elevated majesty facing the costumed peers, the great churchmen and all the members of the House of Commons. The scene looks much the way it did centuries ago, and serves as another dramatic example of how the past still lives in Britain.

The Prince Consort and the Crown Prince

The distinguished looking man often seen walking just behind the queen during many ceremonial occasions is her husband, Prince Philip, the Prince Consort. Sometimes people wonder why he has that title instead of king. Traditionally, the crown has passed by heredity to the first-born sons of the royal family. Should the first-born son die, the second-born son inherits it. The crown is passed to a female only when no direct male heirs exist. The last king of England, George VI, Elizabeth's father, had two daughters, Elizabeth and Margaret, and no sons. Since Elizabeth then inherited the crown, her husband could not have a similarly exalted status, unless she married a foreign king, which would be very difficult to do constitutionally. Therefore, her husband has the title of prince consort, which confers a special status close to but below that of the monarch. Queen Victoria also had a prince consort, Prince Albert, whose image still adorns certain tobacco cans ("tins" in Britain) to this very day.

The son of Queen Elizabeth and Prince Philip, Prince Charles, is heir to the throne. He will become King Charles III when Elizabeth dies or if she abdicates in his favor so that he can have her job while he is young and vigorous. The next in line to the throne after Charles is his first-born son, Prince William.

In Continental European royal families, the heir apparent is often called the crown prince, while in Britain he is referred to as the Prince of Wales. This comes from no particular Welsh ancestry, but from the fact that royal heirs have traditionally been given the title in a special ceremony at Carnarvon Castle in Wales in order to strengthen the tie between England and Wales.

The German Background of the Royal Family

While not very Welsh, the royal family is very German in ancestry. It is descended from German princelings who ruled in the northern German state of Hanover. Victoria's marriage strengthened the German connection, as did the marriages of several of her children to German dynasts. In fact, when Victoria died in 1901, Kaiser William, the future leader of Germany in World War I, marched behind her funeral cortege in a British uniform. The Kaiser was her nephew, so when World War I broke out, royal cousins fought on opposite sides.

It was only in the first half of this century, when Germany loomed as a united, powerful, threatening rival, that the royal family's German connection became an embarrassment. During the superpatriotic days of World War I, there was such pervasive Germanophobia that even lowly sauerkraut became "liberty cabbage." Responding to this atmosphere, the royal family changed its name from Saxe-Coburg-Gotha to Windsor, a thoroughly English name.

The Ultimate Justification for Monarchy and Heredity: God

In an age of democratic egalitarianism in America and Western Europe, how can the existence of this old, feudal, hereditary right to rule by kings and queens be justified by anyone? There is an old explanation that used to justify all kinds of unequal situations in the European world. To put it simply: Since the truth for the Christian world is found in the Bible, what model of government do we find in its pages? Monarchy: powerful, glorious, magnificent and absolute, because God is a king in the Bible. There are no presidents, congresses and city councils in heaven. If we on earth are supposed to model our fallen and sinful world as best we can upon the heavenly model revealed in the Bible, then the only possible form of government that there can be is monarchy.

This argument leads to another. Because the Bible describes a hierarchy in heaven, involving several ranks composed of archangels, angels, seraphim, etc., the early imitation in feudal Europe justified a set of noble ranks from dukes at the top to barons at the bottom. For the rest of society in general, heredity justified nearly everyone's status or lack of it. Social mobility was hardly known for centuries, so if your father was a peasant, you were supposed to be a peasant or married to one because God chose you to be a peasant's son or daughter. This divine choice permeating all of society went right up to the top, to the royal family, which is almost the only role depending solely on hereditary choice in the last decades of the twentieth century.

According to the outlook of America and contemporary Europe today, heredity is given credit for only a few phenomena in our lives. Everyone agrees that it at least determines how tall we are and what basic skin color we have. Yet today, even eye color and hair color can be artificially modified. In traditional Europe, heredity determined so much more than physical attributes. It determined work roles, status and most aspects of what we lump together as "lifestyle" today.

This was because the belief prevailed that your particular soul was determined by God to reside in a particular body at a particular time, in order to fulfill a particular role. Today only royalty continues to obey such divine command. Therefore, Prince Charles as heir to the throne is justified in having his exalted position, but he is also required to shoulder the responsibilities that the job entails.

The Unique Limited Nature of the British Crown

Every so often the queen, in full regalia, meets the Lord Mayor of London, also in full regalia, in order to ask his permission to enter the City of London, that special and oldest section of metropolitan London where financial centers predominate today. The ceremony points up an old right of the City, namely to be free from royal visits unless the permission of the City's authorities is gained beforehand.

Quaint and strange as it seems today, this ceremony displays the fact that the English crown was limited in ancient days. Many other nations can recall a period in their respective histories when a king or an emperor or a tsar ruled with absolute power, at least in theory. This never occurred in Britain. While one or two inept English monarchs speculated over the right of theoretical absolutism, no British monarch could ever come near to putting autocracy into effect. Those who ruled arbitrarily were abruptly checked: King John by the barons through Magna Carta in 1215; King Charles I, who lost his head to Parliament in 1649; and King James II, who had to flee his throne in disarray in 1688.

A strong and clear lesson of British history thus repeated itself: English monarchs were limited by being beneath the law. This meant that there were certain things that sovereigns could not do, and certain rights possessed by subjects which could not be violated by the state. By the late seventeenth century, such an understanding of the English constitution was stated in a clear, attractive and sophisticated manner by John Locke, whose writings were eagerly read by Jefferson, Madison, Washington and many other founders of the United States, all of whom were profoundly influenced by this concept of British freedom. Belief in limited, constitutional government that respects individual rights is one of the grandest achievements to emerge from the long, troubled and sometimes bloody history of the monarchy in England, an achievement enjoyed by many of the nations of the English-speaking peoples today.

UNDERSTANDING BRITISH POLITICAL PARTIES

The Two-Party System

As a result of complicated historical circumstances, English-speaking societies have been blessed with the prevalence of the two-party system. It is in operation most of the time in Britain, the United States, Canada, Australia and New Zealand. Many other nations of the Western world, such as France and Italy, have had a multiple party system functioning in their legislatures, often bringing forth weaker and less stable coalition governments.

Two parties emerged in Britain as early as the 1670s, the Whigs and the Tories. In the nineteenth century, the Whigs became the Liberals and the

Tories became the Conservatives. Although the Liberal Party dominated in the nineteenth century, it lost its steam in the twentieth, and was replaced as a contender for victory at elections by the Labour Party. Ever since World War II, the Conservatives and Labourites have rotated in office, and while the former party seems more cohesive and dominant, the latter shows some signs of internal weakness and external splitting.

The Conservative Party

In some ways, the Conservative Party in Britain is comparable to the Republican Party in the United States, except that British Conservatives accept most of the provisions of the welfare state. Conservatives are strongly in favor of maintaining the American alliance, which includes reliance upon the nuclear deterrent. Conservatives generally display more old-fashioned nationalism and patriotism than their opponents, and rely more upon the private sector of the economy for votes and campaign funds. Businessmen, various other kinds of middle-class people, from professionals to shopkeepers, and many skilled workers regularly support the Conservatives. The old aristocratic and gentry families that used to be so closely associated with the Conservative Party are far less influential and numerous than might be expected. Conservatives tend to praise individual initiative and characteristics of the old Puritan work ethic. Sometimes they are still called by their old name, Tories.

Conservatives are not reactionaries devoted to bringing back the long gone "good old days." In fact, some political commentators have regarded the modern British Conservative Party as more leftward in

its outlook than American Democrats, largely because
the Conservatives freely accept a substantial component of socialism in British life. Then, too, Margaret
Thatcher, the first female political leader of an important Western nation, is a British Conservative. Conservatives have been dynamic ever since they were led in
the nineteenth century by the brilliant Benjamin Disraeli, a novelist son of a Jewish book dealer. It was he
who modernized the old Tory Party and gained lasting recognition as the founder of the modern Conservative Party. Since Disraeli, Conservatives have come
up with creative legislation that has broadened the
franchise and brought about social reform. Such progressive programs have enabled the Conservative Party to appeal to a broad spectrum of the electorate.

The Labour Party

The Labour Party is a phenomenon of the twentieth century. Today it represents a broad spectrum of
voters and interests, from the center to the left, and
not just the interests of organized labor. The party
was organized at the turn of the century and first
came to power, although weakened by coalitions, in
the 1920s. It was only after World War II that the Labour Party gained solid majorities in Parliament and
vigorous cabinets. In the period from 1945 to 1950,
Clement Attlee's Labour government ushered in the
so-called "quiet revolution" that socialized a substantial sector of the British economy.

Many Labour Party members do call themselves
socialists, but they are very British socialists, meaning
that they are wedded to using the democratic ballot
box for enacting change. Bloodcurdling cries for
violent class struggle and volcanic revolution are sim-

ply not British. British socialists also distance themselves from communism and Marxist interpretations of history. Perhaps the best example of the nature of Labour Party socialism can be seen in the way in which successive Labour governments have stood with the American alliance in confrontation with the Soviet Union. Most recently, of course, the Labour Party has veered away from maintaining the American nuclear deterrent on British territory.

The Labour Party can be compared to the Democratic Party in the United States. Just as Democrats were supposed to pick up the bulk of their votes from what we have called "blue collar" workers, Labour is expected to have its strength in the British working classes and their unions. Even so, substantial numbers of American workers have voted Republican in recent years, just as large numbers of British workers have opted for the Conservatives. Moreover, the traditional "smokestack" manufacturing industries have become less significant in both countries, as all sorts of service and high technology occupations have opened up, confronting all of the parties with new groups of potential voters.

Another similarity between Labour and the Democrats is that both parties have usually favored deeper and faster change than their respective opponents. Each party has also had a far left that has been the ideological home for many discontented intellectuals. In Britain, the outraged intellectuals come from all classes and share anger over the continuation of class privilege and what they perceive as economic exploitation.

The Labour Party has long had a strong alliance with the organized trade unions, which wield considerable power in Britain, particularly through their Trade

Union Congress, or T.U.C., an abbreviation that shows up in British newspapers very frequently. The trade unions organize Labour campaign contributions, and their members participate in various political activities from the grass roots up to the Labour government's Cabinet. There is a marked tendency for the trade unions to be a conservative wing of the Labour Party, and to be conservative in their own way in the economy, meaning that first and foremost they seem to guard arrangements in wages and working conditions jealously.

The Third Party Alliance

One other characteristic that the Labour Party shares with American Democrats is that both parties have a tendency to become badly divided between moderates and leftists. Splinter groups or minority parties do form in the United States from time to time, but they are usually absorbed into one of the two major parties. In Britain, it has not always worked out this way because third parties can come along and eventually replace one of the two major parties. This was the case when the Labour Party replaced the Liberal Party as one of the two major parties early in this century.

Today, another third party is in the field, and it is impossible to tell what its fate will be. Dissident moderate Labourites have joined forces with what remains of the old Liberal Party to form what has been called the Alliance Party. These dissident Labourites call themselves Social Democrats.

CIVIL SERVANTS: ESTEEMED BRITISH BUREAUCRATS

Bureaucrats, whether they deserve it or not, receive a bad press in the United States. They are the butt of countless jokes, usually depicting them as dull, overpaid, insensitive and utterly bogged down in red tape. American politicians regularly target them as the cause of waste and mismanagement in government.

The stereotype is a different one in Britain, where government workers are called civil servants. Working for the government in managerial positions has long had high status and professional dignity associated with it, to the extent that many of the best graduates of Oxford and Cambridge regularly aspire to careers as civil servants. In fact, their status is actually higher than that of lawyers and doctors. The British stereotype for the bureaucrat is that of a dedicated, intelligent, impartial, hard working, self-effacing professional denied by choice of all hope of fame and wealth and toiling for the good of all. They are above politics and are permanent employees, regardless of what party is in power.

Perhaps government workers at the higher levels in the American State Department have some of the esteem that British civil servants enjoy. For a long time, the State Department has had a rather unique reputation for professionalism among Washington's executive agencies. At any rate, this sharp contrast in government workers' stereotypes is clearly one of the cultural differences between Britain and America, and travelers in Britain ought to be aware of it.

SENSITIVE AREAS IN POLITICS

There are sensitive political subjects in all countries, which the visitor had better know something about. Just as the traveler in Germany should know something about the Nazi era, and the visitor to South Africa should be familiar with "multi-national development" and the "homelands policy," current euphemisms for segregation, the American visitor in Britain is at a decided advantage if he or she has some knowledge of certain highly sensitive areas in that country today.

Ireland and England

Anyone who has gone through a divorce has an understanding of Anglo-Irish relations. The exaggerated outpourings of resentments, the inability to see both sides, and the resolute, even ferocious determination to be separate that occur in so many divorces often can be observed when people in Ireland or people in Britain talk about the other island. The visitor is in a similarly difficult situation as a friend of a divorcing couple. If you are not entirely for one side, you are likely to be immediately suspected of being for the other side. Sometimes visitors are confronted with the choice of seeing the "Irish problem" in English history or seeing the "English problem" in Irish history.

Whatever it is called, a deep problem exists in the history of each country, going all the way back to the conquest of Ireland by the Anglo-Normans in the twelfth century. Thereafter, old Gaelic or Celtic Irish culture was overcome by English culture, century after century, district after district, spreading out from the most anglicized area right around Dublin. The re-

placement of the native Irish language by English is in-
dicative of this cultural imposition. Today only the
more remote and rural parts of Ireland, basically the
western fringe of the island, speak Gaelic. Yet when
the Reformation changed the religion of most of the
English in Ireland, the native population generally
continued to adhere to the Roman Catholic Church.
Later on, Irish nationalism would rise from this religious base.

In a way, Ireland was a colony supporting an alien
Protestant English aristocracy, but in another way it
was an outlying British area, just as Wales or Scotland
were. Certainly wave after wave of exploiters from
England produced descendants who became very Irish
with the passage of time.

By the nineteenth century, it became clear that
Ireland suffered from a unique dilemma. It was too
close to Britain physically and too connected to Britain
in economics to develop as a separate dominion, the
way in which New Zealand, Canada and Australia became independent nations in the nineteenth century.
On the other hand, the Roman Catholic religion, Celtic culture and the Irish nationalism arising from these
sources made it too difficult for Ireland to subside into
an unequal union with England. Scotland and Wales
had been able to do this, although nationalists from
these places are apt to disagree with this characteriza-
tion.

Many concessions and would-be solutions for this
"Irish problem" were put forth by the British Parliament, but none of them came soon enough or went
far enough for Irish patriots, who pushed for independence. "Home rule" was the solution proposed by
British and Irish liberals, in actuality the status of a
largely self-governing dominion. Just before World

War I, when it seemed near fruition, this solution crashed on the adamant resistance of the Protestants in Northern Ireland.

The "Orangemen," thickly settled in the northern province of Ulster, wanted no part of an Irish dominion that would have a Roman Catholic majority rule Ireland. Orangemen were descended from Scottish settlers who arrived in the seventeenth century, and were Presbyterian or Anglican. In the American colonial period, these people provided hardy frontier pioneers who became known as the Scots-Irish.

While the war clouds darkened over Europe in 1914, Orangemen prepared to fight a civil war against home rule. Two years later, while the First World War was grinding along, Irish Republicans rose in a futile but highly inspirational manner in the Easter Rising of 1916. The brutal British overreaction fanned the flames for an independent Irish republic instead of the more moderate concession, home rule.

A nasty civil war followed between the British and the republicans, and after that, among the republicans themselves. In order to achieve an independent "Irish Free State," some republicans signed a treaty that partitioned Ireland by separating six counties from Ulster, and allowed them to continue as Northern Ireland, still a part of Great Britain.

The Orangemen in these six counties of Northern Ireland see themselves as a nationality sharply distinct from the Catholic Irish. While they see themselves as British, they do not see themselves as merely transplanted Scots or English. To them, to be Northern Irish is to belong to a separate national type, and as such to have the right of national self-determination. This was acknowledged by the partition of Ireland, but the fatal hitch in this scheme was that a very substantial minority in Northern Ireland — up to 40 percent of the population — were Roman Catholics. The Catholic Irish naturally wanted to link up with the Republic of Ireland in the south. To make matters worse, the Orange majority flagrantly discriminated against the Roman Catholics in housing, jobs and social services. Such discrimination led to a Roman Catholic civil rights movement, originally led by Bernadotte Devlin, and when this movement met brutal repression, the area exploded in civil war. The struggle goes on to this day, having claimed thousands of victims from both sides.

The British role in this conflict is extremely sensitive, costly and painful, so visitors are cautioned against snap judgments and simple solutions. For example, the most infuriating of simple solutions can be seen spray-painted all over Ireland and Britain: "Brits out." It implies that if the British would only withdraw from all of Ireland, the situation would subside and peace would finally come to Ireland.

Certainly all the British taxpayers and those British parents, siblings and wives who have loved ones in the British army in Northern Ireland earnestly wish that "Brits out" would be possible. If British forces did withdraw at this stage, a civil war on a much grander scale would probably flare, causing horrible suffering for the innocent on both sides. Moreover, Britain has a legitimate commitment to Northern Ireland, no matter how difficult and stubborn some of their leaders have turned out to be. The Northern Irish contributed heroically in blood and toil to the British war effort in the twentieth century. Can the British desert these people who call themselves British now, especially in light of treaty arrangements pledging the British to underwrite the maintenance of peace and order in the area?

There are no simple solutions. The Orangemen in the North are dead set against joining the republic to the South, fearing that the Roman Catholic Church would impose control over personal lives in matters such as birth control, abortion and divorce. What it comes down to is that four million Catholic Irish cannot force one million unwilling Protestant Irish into a union they will not accept.

Unfortunately, both the Orange and the Roman Catholic Irish have terribly long memories, and will conjure horror tale after horror tale about what the other side has done. Militants on both sides champion the use of violence. Of course, they always plead that they are merely responding to violence, defending themselves, etc., but the fact is that many think that the only way to deal with the other side is with force and violence. Until these basic, brutal, primitive feelings change, British, Protestant Irish and Roman Catholic Irish will continue to bury their dead in vain.

The Irish situation today is the latest chapter in a tragedy that has gone on for centuries. Americans in Britain are well advised to treat it with restraint. Be very careful about responding to discussion about the situation. Snap judgments, flip assumptions, jolly partisanship can all label the visitor as a boor quite quickly. Instead, listen, ask questions, try to savor the complexities, try to measure the depth of the passions involved and try to empathize with the grief expressed. In other words, play the kindly listener to a party in a painful divorce.

The Falkland Islands War

In world history, the Falkland Islands War can be

considered a brief, remote and insignificant contest between Britain and Argentina over bleak islands inhabited by less than two thousand wind-blown settlers whose main preoccupation was and is sheep farming. American visitors had best not make light of this struggle, however, because most Britons hold a serious regard for what they perceived to be at stake.

From a British point of view, a democracy went to war because a military dictatorship had ruthlessly invaded small islands against the wishes of their inhabitants. Britain went to war over a principle, namely that the Falkland Islanders had a right to be British if they wanted to be British. Americans must be cautious in realizing that Britain did not act as a colonial power in violation of the Monroe Doctrine. Regardless of the geographical location of the Falkland Islands, only a handful of Argentinians or Chileans were on the island. Well over 90 percent of the population was British, and wanted to continue to be nothing but British.

There are good reasons why Americans should take pains to treat the British victory with respect. The British have a tendency to hark back to their most recent days of glory, to the time when they stood in defiance of a ring of fascist military dictatorships during World War II. It was easy for them to identify the Argentine invaders with their fascist foes of 1940.

The British were also responding to a perception that several other governments have pushed their nation around in recent years. It seemed time to draw the line and hold it with stubborn British resolution. This was done at some cost. Thereby a message was sent to all nations about Britain's willingness to continue to fight for principles. The Chinese eyeing Hong Kong and the Spanish eyeing Gibraltar were especially invited to take notice.

It had been a long time since the British fought a war in their grandfathers' fashion, that is, by supporting right over might, by sending the fleet, by hanging on with bulldog tenacity and, finally, by seeing the enemy collapse and run up the white flags. When the bands thundered down Whitehall to the tune of "The British Grenadiers," any Anglophile could agree that the British really needed that victory, if only to reaffirm their glorious past.

The Anglo-American Alliance

The very closeness of Britain and America can become a sensitive issue in political discussion in Britain when members of either nationality criticize aspects of it. In the twentieth century, the Anglo-American alliance forged in two World Wars has continued with the same strength in peacetime, and stands as the keystone of the foreign policy of both nations. Of course, there is some irony in the fact that American nationalism originated from fighting Great Britain in the Revolutionary War and the War of 1812. Nevertheless, in this century, no nation is apt to support us more vigorously than Britain, whether at the United Nations or when the United States is embroiled overseas. British support during the Iranian hostage crisis and during the 1986 conflict with Libya are cases in point. We can count on them and they can count on us.

Limits to the alliance show up from time to time, naturally. This can be seen, for example, in the tiff over the American invasion of Grenada. Lack of American support for the British and French invasion of the Suez area in 1956 was a more serious disagreement. It is true that the alliance seems stronger when the British Conservatives are in power. Recently, the

Labour Party took a stand against American nuclear weapons. Yet even when these limitations are taken into account, the Anglo-American alliance still remains the most solid, voluntary, international arrangement of this type in the world today.

There are many good reasons for this solidarity. A shared language is an obvious reason. So is the strong ethnic connection. Roughly half of the population of the United States can trace most of its ancestors to the British Isles. The ancestors of the other half come from everywhere else, Africa to Asia to Continental Europe to Latin America. More significantly, the truly important values and ideals of Britain and the United States are very similar. They think along parallel lines with us about such topics as right and wrong, justice, individual rights and liberties, limitations on government's encroachment on personal freedoms and how people should live under government by laws and not by men. All sorts of legal safeguards for personal freedom, specifically the Bill of Rights, trial by jury and habeas corpus, evolved out of the English experience in history and were taken up by British Americans once the Atlantic colonies were established. To put it succinctly, both societies are supposed to adhere to due process rather than the naked use of power. Both societies, ideally at least, shun the Machiavellian view that the ends justify the means.

After 1945, the United States began to take over the historic role of Britain throughout the world. Today we have bases everywhere, fleets in all oceans and aircraft on patrol on the vast periphery of the Eurasian land mass. Large numbers of Americans work overseas, some in American businesses and some in programs to aid and develop countries. American products and influence are just as ubiquitous as Amer-

ican people. Whenever a serious crisis erupts anywhere, American involvement quickly manifests itself.

All of this American activity may be seen as something of a twentieth century version of the British Empire. Whether or not a person agrees or disagrees with
the propriety of the wide deployment of United States
influence overseas, the role of a great world power is
being assumed, just as the British assumed it in the
Victorian era. Britain was a very small island to command a quarter of the world's people, a quarter of the
earth's land surface and most of the salt water regions.
Yet such was the British achievement in the
nineteenth century. By comparison, America seems so
much larger and so much more suitable for the world
power role, at least at first glance. The important
thing for Americans to bear in mind always is that 95
out of every 100 persons on this globe are not Americans. Therefore, considering our numbers, American
activities overseas are not that dissimilar from the pro-
digious efforts of the British Victorians.

Still adept at diplomacy, banking and foreign affairs, the British help us play the role of world power
in countless subtle and direct ways. They are to us
what the Greeks were to the Romans: the suppliers of
brains and expertise to a powerful imperial people.
This Anglo-American combination has been truly formidable in world affairs in our century.

The American Revolution and the War of 1812

How might the American wars against Britain
commencing in 1776 and 1812 be reconciled with the
existence of the strong twentieth century Anglo-American alliance? This subject may come up for Americans
in Britain; therefore, some views of these struggles

from modern scholarship might be helpful.

First of all, recall that when the bicentennial was celebrated, Britain put on a lavish display celebrating the American Revolution. For them, as well as for Anglophile Americans, the American Revolution was really a civil war, with a pro-revolutionary and an anti-revolutionary faction on both sides of the Atlantic. Besides, Americans fought for traditional English freedoms that had been assured to Englishmen through their own heroic seventeenth century civil war struggles against Charles I, an arbitrary Stuart king. The cry of "no taxation without representation" was first voiced against him, long before the Americans took it up. For pro-revolutionaries, George III assumed the role of Charles I in the American Revolution, although it is known through historical hindsight that a majority in a rather corrupt British Parliament was equally responsible for handling the colonists arbitrarily.

Famous Britons such as William Pitt the Elder, Edmund Burke and John Wilkes championed the colonists' struggles, while in America at least a third of the population was what the British still chose to call "United Empire Loyalists." We call them Tories. Estimates have it that another third in America was either neutral or would side with whichever force was in power locally. What it comes down to is that the active revolutionaries were really a minority of the population in America.

The War of 1812 was a different matter. Americans trace a good deal of their early nationalism to this struggle. It was, after all, the occasion to write our national anthem. For the British, it was a minor sideshow in the larger, desperate struggle to defeat Napoleon's France. They see it as a victory for themselves, or at least a draw. It involved a successful defense of Canada from Yankee greed and featured the capture and burning of the American capital. The most stinging British defeat, Andrew Jackson's celebrated victory at New Orleans, was tragically fought after the war had been concluded by a treaty drawn up by diplomats in Europe.

It was fortunate for the later relations of Britain and America that both of these wars were not marred by the brutality and ferocity that have come to mark civil wars in the twentieth century. There were hardly any atrocities against men in uniform or against civilians. The leaders on both sides behaved like gentlemen because they were gentlemen. To be sure, tarring and feathering is most unpleasant, but is it milder than the punishment meted out to most suspected traitors or collaborators in our century. When the British were defeated in the American Revolution, the losers' friends were not lined up against a wall and shot, the fate so often meted out to the losers in twentieth century revolutions. Defeated Tories could go to Canada, Bermuda, or back to Britain. Most actually located elsewhere in America, perhaps closer to the frontier, where they could cover up their past loyalty to Britain. Who knows how many Daughters of the American Revolution are actually descended from these former Tories?

When visiting Britain, it is best to be generous when the topic of the American Revolution comes up. Treat it as a civil war. Do not stress how the British lost the war. Instead, point out that they, too, were winners because the best elements of British society, the reformers, were on the side of the Americans. After 1783, these reformers were eventually able to correct many abuses and glaring corruptions of the old parliamentary system. Therefore, the American Revolution can be seen as a victory for representative government on both sides of the Atlantic. By the way, if the American visitor can pull off this interpretation of the American Revolution, he or she will be a long way towards mastering the British art of diplomacy.

Race and Racial Disturbances

Americans are highly sensitive to racial issues. One important reason is that one out of eight descends, at least in part, from slaves whose status was denigrated by race. Middle-aged Americans remember the struggle for civil rights first hand, and the segregation that went on so blatantly before that. Most Americans are aware that some of the saddest topics in American history involve the brutal effects of racism and bigotry.

It therefore comes as something of a shock to read of racial disturbances in Britain, complete with looting, burning and accusations of police brutality. Some cynics say that whatever comes to the United States will eventually arrive in Britain, and urban racial disturbances are another example of this phenomenon. Bigots blame the heavy post-war immigration of blacks from former British possessions for causing these scenes in hitherto peaceful Britain.

American visitors should be forearmed with some perspective on these kinds of disturbances in Britain. First of all, there have been many periods of ethnically inspired riots and disturbances going all the way back in the country's history. They involved Jews, Germans, Irish, Scots and, going far into the past, even Vikings and Romans. Secondly, in the recent riots, the overall scale of racial violence was much lower than has been the case in the United States. Thirdly, the racial composition of the British rioters was somewhat mixed, and the issues of discrimination protested against did not seem to be as clearly racially based as they have been in the United States.

Behind these differences may be the essentially different history of blacks in Britain. A decision handed down by a British judge in the latter eighteenth century declared that the instant a slave set foot in Britain, he or she was a free person. This is, by the way, just the opposite of the notorious Dred Scott decision in United States history. So the blacks who came to Britain during the time that slavery flourished in America were all free. They tended to be servants and seamen, and with the passage of time they blended into the British population undramatically.

After World War II, substantial numbers of blacks and Asians came to Britain from newly independent former colonial areas to seek employment and a better way of life. Nevertheless, the percentage of non-whites did not exceed five percent, a much smaller percentage than that of the black population in the United States. Even so, the presence of a substantial non-white population in Britain, concentrated in London and a few other places, was a relatively new phenomenon.

Behind American race relations are the tragedies of slavery, segregation and bloody repressions of civil rights. The American Civil War and the Reconstruction Era were major traumas in United States history. There is nothing parallel to this in the British experience, so it is not realistic to predict American patterns for future developments in race relations in Britain.

Americans are often shocked by blatant, overt racism in Britain, since bigots in the United States have largely become closet bigots. Racism in Britain is often outspoken and crude, whether shouted by poor East London cockneys or smoothly enunciated by Enoch Powell, a student of the classics and member of Parliament. In a way, this racism is an angry reaction against change. In another way, it is a manifestation of that age-old British xenophobia, or fear of foreigners. British verbal skills at getting to the point and emphasizing it unambiguously undoubtedly contribute to Americans' frequent dismay at the tone of British racism.

On the other hand, there is an old British tradition which affirms that all people of all backgrounds in race, creed and origin can become British. Being British is hard to define, but it consists of a certain civilized behavior, a certain openness of mind and a certain sense of fair play. Therefore, from this point of view, a population of "Black British" exists, and visiting Americans should not make the mistake, as they very often do, of thinking of the British as whites only. The bigots, cockney or sophisticated, can all be matched by other Britons who are tolerant, accepting and appreciative of superficial physical differences among humans. They appreciate the malleability of cultural backgrounds in a British environment. They know that the great civilizations of history have been world civilizations, capable of inspiring the loyalties of varieties of people. At its best, British civilization is such; at its worst, it is insular and narrow minded. The visitor will see both aspects.

Gun Control

Gun control can become a sensitive issue for Americans in Britain because the British are likely to express interest in the subject to elicit a conversation.

They know that opinion in America is bitterly divided on the subject.

Gun control is no issue in Britain. Laws are strict and severe: Handguns are completely banished and other guns can only be used for sport. When not in use, they are to be kept broken down and in a locked receptacle subject to regular police inspection. Nearly no one in Britain either owns or wants to own a gun. Even criminals traditionally prefer knives because they are less dangerous, although, sadly, this is changing. Moreover, only certain crack units of the British police use guns. The rest do without, relying instead upon the authority of the law, cheerfulness, common sense and a short, heavy truncheon (nightstick in the U.S.) that they keep tucked away somewhere in their uniforms. The ordinary London "bobby" stands in sharp contrast to the American policeman whose arsenal of gun, mace, club and handcuffs dangles from his exterior menacingly.

If anything truly appalls and frightens the British about America, it is the homicidal carnage brought about through the indiscriminate use of handguns. Indeed, a person's chance of being a homicide victim is something on the order of 20 times greater in the United States than in Britain.

Some interpretation of this alarming statistic is necessary. While homicides in America are widespread, they cluster most heavily in the inner city areas, where minority citizens are the most common victims and the most common perpetrators. Poverty and the deprived environment in which it festers can be cited as the root cause. The easy availability of handguns and the long American tradition of gun use certainly contribute considerably to the toll of homicides. For the rest of the country, the availability of handguns and the cultural traditions of having them handy make murder and accidental shooting commonplace events in all kinds of American environments.

Americans who point to the right to bear arms in the Constitution will be countered by Britons who declare that this right is also in their Constitution. They will insist that they can still bear arms if they want to, but only according to strict rules, rules from laws passed by their democratic legislature.

Clearly, American visitors in Britain will be on the defensive if they choose to debate the issue from the pro-gun standpoint of the National Rifle Association. By contrast, those Americans who are for banning handguns will feel that British life goes a long way to prove their point.

Crime and Violence in America

Another sensitive area for Americans in Britain involves the high incidence of crime and violence in the U.S. Stories circulate all over Britain about such things as British tourists being mugged in Miami or New York by gun-toting, minority group adolescents. The more discerning British know that there are certain high risk areas in all American cities, places that have fantastically high crime rates and thereby skew all of the crime statistics for America. It remains up to the American visitor to explain to the less discerning Briton that there are many quiet, peaceful towns and vast stretches of generally law-abiding suburbia where crime and violence are much more exceptional.

Even when all of this is pointed out, it must be admitted that the United States is a far more violent society than Britain and other western European nations. Ghetto crime, family violence, violent thefts and

violence for the sheer sadistic fun of it are all too
prevalent. Americans agonize over solutions. Some
wish to get tough with criminals, overlooking the fact
that the U.S. already vies with South Africa and the
Soviet Union in having the highest percentage of citizens warehoused in jail. Others call for campaigns of
public effort to combat the unemployment and neglect
that they see as the cause of violent crime. Whatever
they perceive as causes and proposed solutions, Americans are divided and vulnerable. British people want
to probe the subject because they believe that their
own society is becoming more violent, and they want
to know more about its causes in America.

Fears of American violence have another dimen-
sion in British minds. Irresponsible, trigger-happy
foreign policies are imputed to Americans quite readily. In recent years Barry Goldwater, Alexander Haig
and Ronald Reagan were each the cause of considerable concern in Britain for fear that their militant nationalism might lead to war.

The actual causes of the high incidence of
violence in America are, of course, complex and difficult to unravel. Here is a viewpoint that might be
worth advancing by an American visitor in Britain: It
certainly has something to do with the mystique of the
frontier, where the heroic cowboy stereotype used
guns and fists to win the West. Force and violence
won for such good guys, the prototypes for John
Wayne and Gary Cooper, so force and violence ought
to win for their American cultural heirs today. Behind
this is the belief that God helps the righteous in mortal
combat, an attitude reinforced deep down in everybody born before 1940 or so by victory over evil in
World War II. It can be argued that until recently,
American males have been under some pressure to

demonstrate their strength and determination in displays of physical courage. Relatively recently, the war in Vietnam and the sexual revolution's varied manifestations have fundamentally shaken the old stereotypes from the American past. Nevertheless, since America is a huge and complex society, there are many John Wayne imitators still crushing beer cans and shouting hoarse defiance to the world.

Awkward Exceptions over Sensitive Areas

Britain has long been a place where freedom of thought and expression have been given free play, so expect to find dazzling nonconformity. Just as some people delight in wearing outrageous fashions in this free country, others deliberately extol positions that go against the grain of the majority. The visitor who has done his homework in scouting British opinions often finds that his efforts have done him little good when confronted by a loud and flamboyant extremist. For example, the visitor might be told that what is really necessary for Northern Ireland is that the Brits should get out, or that the Falklands should be surrendered to Argentina immediately or that the Anglo-American alliance is all rubbish and that the United States should revert to isolationism again and leave the rest of the world alone. What is so often engaging about these blatant British nonconformists is that they may use wonderfully persuasive English to present weak arguments. The main thing for the challenged visitor to do in such a confrontation is to stay level headed, be good natured, and keep a sense of humor at play. Getting very angry and shouting will blow it, creating what the British call a "wind up," which is pronounced "wined" and means that someone has been overly flustered. It is precisely the reaction that many nonconformists are looking for. These are the ones who get their jollies from wind ups.

CHAPTER FIVE

Understanding British History

INTRODUCTION: THE PRESENCE OF HISTORY

The visitor from the United States, particularly from the West, might find the impact of history delightfully overwhelming. This is because this crowded, small island has been populated by dynamic and creative people for so very many centuries. The cumulative effect of era built upon era and style following style can bewilder. History is present everywhere, in houses, inns, walls, churches, parks, cathedrals, castles, names, customs, institutions, costumes, entertainment, roads, lanes, fields, ruins, sites, decorations, honors and ceremonies. Above all, it is in the minds of many of its living heirs.

Americans from the East Coast are probably better at dealing with such historical richness than

Americans from the West. After all, how much history can there be in a place that might have been settled for only a bit more than a century? So much of the West looks rather devoid of history, as if everything is fairly new. In many cases, this is because of a tendency to despise and destroy what is from the past and to rebuild according to the latest fashion. For example, in some of the burgeoning cities on the Front Range of Colorado, the steel ball of demolition regularly smashes some of the very few remaining Victorian and Edwardian buildings so that new gas stations, condominiums or quickie foods emporiums can spring from the ruins. These atrocities are sometimes called "progress" by developers.

Certainly the destruction of the past for the profits of the present occurs in Britain also, and there are similar disagreements between the historical preservationists and the developers. Yet there are differences. In Britain, the laws are more stringent and regularly enforced. It is also much harder to demolish the past because the people maintain a widespread and deep love for it. They treasure their history. Another difference is that British people share with Europeans mastery of the art of renovation. They adapt the treasures of the past for modern life. For instance, electric lights and modern plumbing can be fitted into a comfortable five-hundred-year-old house that is expected to last at least another five-hundred years.

This chapter gives a brief overview of all of British history. Bear in mind that the topics are as familiar to British people as the Civil War and the first Thanksgiving are to Americans. This overview ought to provide a helpful orientation because it is inevitable that a good deal of this material will come up during a visit to Britain.

PREHISTORIC BRITAIN

A vast stretch of British history is prehistoric because history does not begin until there are written records. The Romans were the first to provide them for Britain, beginning around a half century before the birth of Christ. All that came before was prehistoric, just as everything before 1492 is prehistoric for America.

What we know about prehistoric times still remains largely shadowy and sketchy. Folklore abounds. It was the time of the Druids, mysterious priests and great female warriors who went to battle in chariots.

"England before the English" is one description of the era because the English were the Anglo-Saxons, and they did not arrive until the period from the 400s to the 600s A.D. Various other people invaded and subdued the island of Britain during this period. The most famous of all the prehistoric people to do so were the Celts. Today considerable numbers of their descendants and Celtic cultural attributes are to be found in Scotland, Wales and the West Country. They are related to the Celts of Ireland and Brittany, in France.

There are several impressive sites in Britain that indicate the profound efforts of what were very thin prehistoric populations. Many are in the form of megaliths, or specially arranged large stones. Stonehenge is the most famous of these sites, standing bold and magnificent on the plains near Salisbury. A recent computerized study has confirmed earlier speculation that Stonehenge was built for the purpose of sun worship. Visitors who go to Stonehenge will invariably find fellow Americans wandering about at the site, since it is very popular with our tourists.

ROMAN BRITAIN

It is difficult to conceive of a period when Britain was a remote frontier area rather than a vital center of civilization. Yet this was precisely the case during the surprisingly long period when the far-flung Roman Empire prevailed over Britain. The Romans ruled this wet and cold frontier region far from their sunny Mediterranean center for 400 years, from 43 B.C. to 450 A.D. or so.

Despite the length of time that the Romans occupied Britain, the net effect of their civilization on Britain was largely negligible. The main reason for this is that the Anglo-Saxons flooded into Roman Britain in such numbers and with such barbaric force from the fifth century onwards that they largely obliterated the Roman civilization on the island. Today, the substantial physical remains of Rome in Britain, mostly ruins and excavated sites, are more significant for understanding Roman history than for understanding British history because there is no spiritual inheritance from Rome. Even the important Latin component of the English language came from Norman French, not Roman Latin.

The Romans left testimony to their skill in engineering all over Britain. Stretching across the narrow nick of northern England is Hadrian's Wall, a massive defensive barrier designed to keep the fierce northern peoples out of Roman Britain. Many sections of it remain today in extremely impressive form. Roman villas, temples, baths, floors and statuary have been dug up here and there by archaeologists. In many places, Roman structures were incorporated right into medieval walls, gates and roads, a tribute to the fact that the Romans built things to last.

Two Romanized Britons are famous. Both lived in the shadowy world during the barbarian onslaughts at the very end of the Roman period. One of them, St. Patrick, is famous for Christianizing Ireland. The other, King Arthur, has wrongly gone down in history as a Christian king who supposedly lived when knighthood was in flower. Actually, Arthur was an upholder of Roman, Christian civilization against the invading Anglo-Saxon pagans.

ANGLO-SAXON ENGLAND, 450-1066

There is an irony about the whole Anglo-Saxon period. Momentous developments occurred, yet very little physical evidence of this long era in English history remains. The ethnic change was profound. The beginning of the era was truly the "Dark Ages" for Britain because masses of Germanic people migrated to the plain of England from Germany and the Low Countries and drove the Celts into the hills of the West Country and Wales. This new dominant population, generally tall and blond, would become the basic ethnic stock for the rest of English history. Their Germanic language evolved into English, a fact revealed when comparing everyday words in English with everyday words in German. For example, "Fuss" in German is "foot" in English; "Tür" in German is "door" in English, and so on. Of course, after 1066 the Normans brought a rich addition of Latin-based French to this Germanic speech.

The Anglo-Saxons achieved a great deal before the Normans arrived. They mastered the landscape, felling forests and plowing up heavy clay soils with iron tools. During their long rule of England, they underwent a transformation from pagan barbarians to civilized, medieval Christians who developed a remarkable system of common law which operated on the basis of a high degree of community involvement.

The evolution of several Anglo-Saxon kingdoms in Britain was interrupted by ferocious Viking invasions. A Christian hero, Alfred, King of Wessex, resisted these Scandinavians heroically. Eventually the Vikings and their descendants were Christianized and blended into the population. They were particularly numerous in the northeast of England, in a region called Danelaw when they controlled it.

The American connection to Anglo-Saxon England is substantial. Our language, our law, important elements of our institutions and a substantial proportion of our ethnic stock are derived from the Anglo-Saxons. Their world was a world of the forest frontier, so when a new frontier beckoned in North America, Anglo-Saxon ways and customs proved to be immensely useful, even down to using sheriffs (called shire reeves originally) and posses.

Despite their tremendous achievements over this 600-year span of English history, relatively few Anglo-Saxon buildings and parts of buildings remain. Naturally, for the first centuries of their occupation of England, the Anglo-Saxons were simply becoming civilized, and had not yet developed architecture in stone. Later they did, but it is not so easy for the visitor to get in touch with the Anglo-Saxon past. Therefore, any evidence of the Anglo-Saxon past that he or she may come across is to be relished, no matter how unspectacular it may first appear to be.

MEDIEVAL BRITAIN, 1066-1485

The Setting of the Times

Medieval is the adjective for the Middle Ages, the thousand years stretching from the end of the ancient world to the Renaissance era, roughly the 400s to the 1400s. The Anglo-Saxon period falls into it, but because this was such a unique era in British history, it has been treated separately from the rest of medieval Britain.

The medieval era has been called the "Age of Faith," and it can be argued that never before or never since have religious beliefs so dominated the mind of Western civilization. It was an epoch when the great cathedrals were erected; when new religious orders were founded; when friars, monks, nuns, monasteries and convents were prominent everywhere; when all those who taught at the universities were in holy orders; and when the church had the responsibility to run the hospital and welfare systems.

The works of faith were only one side of the medieval world. Incessant warfare among armed kings, nobles, knights and retainers added notes of violence and instability. Medieval kings tended to be weaker than later on, unless they were particularly able men, as a consequence of the feudal system, wherein they were bound to contractual roles with powerful lords. Poor transportation and communication detracted from royal power also. Civil war was apt to flare up in the kingdom when a minor came to the throne, or when a particularly feeble king inherited the throne, or when the succession was disputed.

The size and strength of castles attest to the power that medieval nobles possessed. Some were clearly what were called "over-mighty subjects," whose domains bristled with armed retainers. The basis of noble power rested upon the possession of numerous manors, or medieval feudal estates. Upon them worked the masses of impoverished agricultural workers, the peasants and serfs who made up the overwhelming majority of the population. The manor, the nearby local church and the village comprised their entire world, for in most cases they were bound to it, almost in a servile state.

Feudalism was an economic, political and social system that allocated these manors and the peasants who went with them to a militaristic elite. The manors produced the economic surplus that kept this elite of knights and lords well armed and free to pursue war as a profession. The knights were specialists at war who operated, along with the lords above them, in a complex web of rights and obligations, most of which were sanctioned by the church. At best, feudalism sought to protect the church and peasants from violence; at worst, it exploited the masses so that the aristocratic sport of war could have full indulgence.

Romantic writers have embellished the Middle Ages. Troubadours, heroic knights, damsels in distress, mysterious prisoners in dungeons and the whole panoply of chivalry have been exalted. In actuality, the medieval period was dark, filthy, dank, nasty and miserable for at least 95 percent of the population. Death came early to many people of all classes, and sometimes it came in wholesale form, as a plague.

Grim as these times were for most people, there are many striking medieval achievements of a lasting nature. Significant permanent institutions originated and evolved, including Parliament and the great ancient universities, Oxford and Cambridge. Parliament's development has been cited as the greatest achievement of the age because it shaped the development of the rest of English history. "England made a Parliament and her Parliament made England" is how it is put in a popular saying. Other countries had medieval representative bodies also, but what was special about England's Parliament was that two houses developed, one for lords and the other for knights and burgesses, prominent leaders from the countryside and towns, respectively. Since they were non-noble, they were commoners at law, hence the name "House of Commons." In the Middle Ages, the function of Parliament was usually to help the monarch to govern his realm. With strong kings, the regal voice was amplified by Parliament. It was only later on, in the seventeenth century, that the House of Commons would challenge monarchs for authority.

The Norman Conquest

European style feudalism was first imposed upon England by the Normans, who carried out a swift, bloody and brutal conquest of England, beginning in 1066. The Normans kept much of the society and institutions of Anglo-Saxon England intact, but they imposed themselves as an alien elite all over the country. Everywhere, defeated Anglo-Saxon nobles were replaced by French-speaking conquerors. The language still bears evidence of their impact. Words of French origin still predominate for the topics of diplomacy, war, politics, cooking, hunting and in the realm of what we can call interpersonal subtleties. By any measure, 1066 was a landmark year in English history — the year when William I of Normandy, known as William the Bastard, defeated the last Anglo-Saxon king,

Harold, at the battle of Hastings. Who were these Normans who rapidly imposed French feudalism and church organization on England? They came from Normandy, a seacoast province of France, but they were non-French in origin. These seething, restless conquerors were Frenchified Scandinavians, called Northmen originally, who had come south to conquer Normandy only just over a hundred years before launching their conquest of England. The number that came with William initially was quite few, for only 8,000 disembarked to fight the fateful battle of Hastings.

Once in authority, the Normans energetically transformed the superstructure of England. They left their hallmarks in massive stone architecture. Many cathedrals, churches and castles today boast of their Norman portions or foundations. Massive Norman arches and columns are unmistakable, and testify to the sheer power of these people.

The Normans were the very last conquerors of England, and they did the job with thoroughness. They were never overthrown. Instead, they were absorbed over a few centuries by a two-way cultural and biological diffusion.

Significant Post-Conquest Rulers

Medieval kings after William I varied in quality from the awful to the magnificent. For most people, learning about all of the medieval rulers has little point, so what follows is a list of the outstanding, along with their main achievements. English medieval political history is really a tangled skein, so presenting just the minimum number of royal personages might be the most helpful approach.

Henry II (1154-1189) was a vigorous, able monarch who made dramatic improvements in the legal system. He was implicated in the assassination of Thomas à Becket, and this left a blot on his memory. He was married to Eleanor of Aquitaine, and had quarrelsome sons. The play *Lion in Winter* is about his family. Henry II was the king in the film *Becket* which, incidentally, contains some dubious history. Henry II was the first of a line of kings called Plantagenet, a line with strong French connections.

Richard I (1189-1199) is known as Richard the Lionhearted. He spent only a short period of his reign in England because he devoted himself to the Crusades and other adventures abroad. Robin Hood was supposed to have been active when Richard was away. He was one of Henry II's sons.

John (1199-1216), Richard's younger brother, has gone down in history as a villain. He had to sign Magna Carta in 1215, that great historic document which acknowledged legal limitations to royal power. In it, specific liberties of lords and freemen were spelled out in great detail, and subsequent monarchs acknowledged it when they ascended the throne. Through the centuries, Magna Carta was reinterpreted again and again, so that eventually due process, the right to trial by jury and the right to be represented in a legislature all came to be read into the document.

Henry V (1413-1422) had a short but glorious reign. He fought the French with dash and heroism, achievements celebrated by Shakespeare in the play named after this monarch.

Richard III (1483-1485), in the hands of Shakespeare, has gone down as one of the worst villains in English history, an ugly, vicious and greedy usurper who was responsible for murdering two little princes in the Tower of London. Debate still simmers over just how evil or misjudged this monarch was.

Famous English Medieval Struggles

From Henry II on, England's line of Plantagenet kings had extensive holdings in France and claims to the French throne. Added to England, their territory was called the Angevin Empire. Holding on to French land and claims became a costly preoccupation for English medieval kings. Long struggles with France, collectively called the Hundred Years' War, lasted from around 1338 to 1453. In them, England won grand and glorious battles, such as Agincourt, but lost the war. Joan of Arc emerged at one stage to resist them as a saintly warrior.

In the fifteenth century, the descendants of the Plantagenets fell out among themselves as they sought to capture the throne, aided and abetted by rival factions of powerful nobles. These confusing struggles, involving seven monarchs and lasting from 1399 to 1485, were called the Wars of the Roses. One faction, the House of York, was associated with the white rose, and the red rose was attributed to the House of Lancaster, its rival. The Lancastrians won when Henry VII ascended the throne in 1485, but he smoothed the rivalry over considerably by marrying the heiress of the other side, Elizabeth of York. Therefore, in their son, Henry VIII, both factions were united.

Medieval Castles and Their Lessons

Castles and cathedrals are the two most significant kinds of medieval buildings; one reveals the warlike, struggling nature of the era and the other demonstrates its soaring faith.

Individual tastes in castles vary. Some visitors prefer uninhabited, ruined castles and some prefer those which have been repaired, added to, and inhabited down to the present. Certainly none of England's castles look as they did in the Middle Ages, when bright, pointed turrets flying flags and stuccoed exteriors gave them a Disneyland look. For the best examples of castles fallen into ruin, but with quite a bit still standing, Conway and Harlech in Wales can be recommended. For a castle kept in use until very recently, when it was taken over by the same organization that runs Madame Tussaud's waxworks, Warwick Castle can be recommended.

Castles were strong, defensive structures placed in strategic locations that were intended as royal strongpoints operated by the king's loyal nobles. In actuality, many nobles used their castles against the crown, their castles representing the strength of local, feudal authority instead of the distant monarch. Great, predatory noble families made them their homes and bases of operations in the grand medieval sport of war. Before cannons were developed, a well-stocked and well-garrisoned castle could hold out against extremely long sieges.

The spectacular castles of Wales were English outposts rapidly built in a conquered but still rebellious Welsh tribal countryside. Some of them are still the grandest in all of Britain, despite the ruin they were allowed to fall into after the Middle Ages. The Welsh always saw them as the physical symbols of English domination over them.

Some Helpful Terms for Understanding Castles

A *barbican* is the outer fortification, or the outwork.

A *breastwork* is often a temporary defensive work, breast high.

The *donjon (dungeon)* is the main tower or the keep of the castle. Often the cellar or the deep interior is referred to as the donjon and is the grim place where the prisoners were kept.

The *keep* is usually the strongest part of the castle, designed to be the last place to hold out in a siege.

The *parapet* can be an outer wall.

The *portcullis* is a grating of strong bars of wood or iron that can be suddenly dropped across the gateway of a castle.

The *rampart* is the embankment surrounding a castle upon which the parapet is raised. Sometimes the term includes the parapet.

The *turret* is a small tower rising above the walls. The great castles would have many of them.

Medieval Cathedrals and Their Lessons

It is amazing how medieval cathedrals can still dominate the skylines of British cities in this century of high rises. Even though our age takes massiveness in architecture for granted, the size and the grandeur of old cathedrals remain breathtaking. Each of them is unique, having a different atmosphere and special characteristics. Local people are likely to take ardent pride in their own cathedral, to the extent that they fancy it to be the very best of all the cathedrals in Britain.

If most people lived close to the subsistence level

on manors, how did society muster enough social energy to construct edifices on such a magnificent scale? As with Stonehenge, cathedrals reveal the overwhelming, compelling force of religion. They also attest to the medieval view of the world that regarded life on earth as short and nasty and the life in the world to come in heaven as glorious. The color, artistry, lighting and soaring architecture of the cathedrals gave a foretaste of heaven, and this beauty must have transfixed medieval people with awe and wonder. Each cathedral was rooted in the earth, actually in the middle of masses of graves. The interior and exterior were covered with carvings and statues of all sorts of people and creatures, some saintly, some wicked and some ordinary. Above, towers and spires reached skyward dramatically, touching heaven itself. The edifice consequently embraced all of existence, from death to life and beyond, to life after death. What could be more important to medieval people than to worship God by constructing glorious cathedrals that gave witness to their full relationship with Him?

Despite the uniqueness of each and every cathedral, all have some basic similarities. All are built in the shape of a cross, with the east end pointing towards Jerusalem. Each was the base for the jurisdiction, or diocese, of a bishop. All of the cathedrals were built slowly and painstakingly, often over several centuries. Salisbury cathedral is something of an exception, since it was put up in a relatively short period of time, all in one century! Another similarity is that originally all of the medieval cathedrals were Roman Catholic edifices. It was only with the Reformation in the sixteenth century that they became cathedrals of the Church of England, or Anglican cathedrals. Some of them sustained some damage, destruction and remodeling from the more zealous Protestants thereafter.

Some confusion can arise from this point about the Reformation. Ever since the nineteenth century, Roman Catholic dioceses have been reintroduced into Britain, meaning that new Roman Catholic cathedrals have been built to rival the great, historic Anglican cathedrals as well as the newer ones that the Church of England has built. To confuse things further, Anglicans regularly refer to their church as "catholic," with a small "c," meaning that it is universal, for all people. At the same time, many Anglicans prefer to call themselves Protestant.

Undoubtedly, the twentieth century is proving to be much more destructive of medieval cathedrals than the flare-up of Protestant excesses in the sixteenth and seventeenth centuries. Experts estimate that auto and industrial exhausts have eaten into the stonework to the extent that all the damage of all the previous centuries put together cannot match the destruction of our own century. This explains the many campaigns to fund their preservation. Cleaning and repairing these gigantic structures is such an ongoing struggle that it seems impossible to see any cathedral in Britain without encountering scaffolds over at least one of the major surfaces.

Visitors should take their time in cathedrals. If each took centuries to build, there is no sense in rushing through in fifteen minutes. Purchase a guidebook or use the "Info Bar" phone commentaries and go slowly. You should not try to understand everything in church history, art history or architectural history. That is the way to become overwhelmed. Instead, open yourself to impressions and feelings and savor these buildings and what they contain.

Some Helpful Terms for Understanding Cathedrals

No matter how open the visitor is to impressions and feelings in cathedrals, simply getting around them requires a small, specialized vocabulary. The signs, the "phone bar" information systems and the churchmen who guard the edifices while helping the tourists all use a number of specific terms not often heard in America, largely because this nation lacks European-style cathedrals except for a few places on the East Coast. Below is a list of helpful terms (also see the diagram) to enhance your visit. Basic terms already known in America, such as aisle, altar, arch, dome, spire and steeple, are omitted.

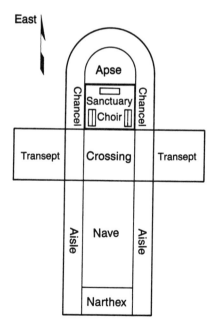

A Simplified Diagram of a Cathedral

Terms for the Floor Plan

The *apse* is a projecting extension of the cathedral, usually semi-circular, with vaults, and in the east end of the building.

The *chancel* is usually to the east of the nave (see below) and includes the choir and the sanctuary.

The *choir* is the part of the chancel between the sanctuary and the nave which is occupied by singers or the clergy.

The *crossing* is the place where the transept and nave intersect. It is usually square.

The *narthex* is the area leading to the nave. It was originally a porch or a vestibule. Now it may be a place for informal conversation, notices or for the selling of souvenirs.

The *nave* is the main west to east body of the cathedral. It usually extends from the main entrance to the choir.

The *sanctuary* is where the altar is placed.

The *transept* comprises the two lateral arms of the cathedral, north to south. These are the arms of the cross shape of the building.

Terms for Decorations, Objects and Some Other Locations

The *altarpiece* is a work of art, often consisting of one or more painted panels, that is placed in a space above and behind the altar.

An *arcade* is a series of arches with their columns, and is often roofed.

A *boss* is a raised or projecting ornament on a wall or ceiling.

A *chapel* within a cathedral is usually a chamber or a recessed area for subordinate services of prayer and meditation. Chapels usually have separately dedicated altars.

A *choir stall* is a seat in the choir, often elaborately decorated and enclosed.

A *cloister* is a covered passageway at the side of an open court, usually walled on the side farthest from the court and colonnaded (having a row of columns) on the other side.

A *crypt* is an area under the main body of a cathedral, underground, and usually utilized for burials.

A *flying buttress* consists of a mass of arches jutting out from an upper wall or vaulted ceiling. Its purpose is to take on the weight of these upper structures. Flying buttresses usually extend themselves out and down on the outside of the cathedral.

The *font* is a receptacle for holy water or baptismal water.

A *fresco* is a wall painting executed on freshly spread plaster.

A *gargoyle* is really a waterspout, made in the form of a grotesque human or animal form. Gargoyles project from buildings and once served to frighten worshippers with images of demons.

A *minster* is a monastery church, and can be an important cathedral as well. York Minster is an example.

A *ribbed vault* is a vault, or arched masonry ceiling, that is supported by a skeleton of compartmentalized arches.

A *sacristy* is a chamber where the vestments, or religious garments, and sacred utensils are stored.

A *see* is the official seat of a bishop and the center of his jurisdiction. His chief church will be the cathedral.

Tracery refers to ornamental designs, often interlaced with branching lines.

Terms Referring to Styles of Decoration

The terms below can become confusing because nearly all cathedrals have additions in different styles from the style of the primary construction. The following terms are arranged in chronological order.

The *Norman* style was executed massively in heavy masonry. Their arches are huge, thick, round and adorned very simply. The Norman style was a variety of the Romanesque style.

Romanesque is the term for the general style of architecture of the early Middle Ages, up to the coming of Gothic style. From the 1000s on, it was characterized by the use of round arches and many arcades.

Gothic was the style of architecture characteristic of the Middle Ages from the twelfth to the sixteenth centuries. It featured tall, slim architectural masses supported by flying buttresses. Ribbed vaulting and pointed arches were other characteristics. In England, three varieties of Gothic style developed:

Early English Gothic was the first version of the Gothic style in England, and was characterized by *lancet* arches, which are narrow arches that come to sharp points.

The *Decorated Style* came next. It was characterized by geometric tracery, or interlaced geometric designs.

The *Perpendicular Style* is the name of the later stage of English Gothic, appearing in the late fourteenth century and onwards. Arches became extremely slender and gracefully pointed.

THE AGE OF THE TUDORS, 1485-1603

A Magnificent Century for England

The age of faith and feudalism, symbolized by cathedrals and castles, gradually faded into the early modern period in Europe during the sixteenth century. In England, the change is marked by the arrival of the House of Tudor in 1485. The Tudors included some of the most magnificent English rulers of all times, and their resplendent age is appreciated far and wide today for its color and romance. It was also the time when many striking women played major roles in history.

Nearly all Americans know something about Henry VIII, Elizabeth I and Shakespeare, and some Americans regard Tudor history as the earliest chapter of American history because it was then that English ships laid claim to the New World, and English monarchs tried to colonize Virginia for the first time.

This magnificent century in English history actually began very inauspiciously as crafty, clever Henry VII barely managed to grasp the crown during the last major round of the Wars of the Roses. He won it at the battle of Bosworth in 1485, defeating Richard III, the last king of the House of York, a monarch who gained an evil and ugly image from the pen of Shakespeare. Henry was an heir of the rival House of Lancaster, yet he was able to marry the most prominent Yorkist heiress, Elizabeth, which guaranteed that all subsequent Tudors would blend the red rose and white rose factions in their heredity.

Henry VIII and His Times

Henry VIII has always been controversial. Who was the real Henry VIII — the charming, talented Renaissance prince or the vicious, egotistical tyrant? The debate will never end. In order to secure a legitimate heir, he married six women. He beheaded two of them; divorced two of them; one died; and one outlived him. Along the way, he opened the floodgates of the Reformation in England by breaking with the Roman Catholic Church and becoming the leader of the Church of England, which more or less kept the same buildings and personnel. While he did destroy the monasteries, which was a very Protestant thing to do, much else in the church remained in the catholic manner.

The American equivalent of Church of England is the Episcopal church. Episcopalians have considerable difficulty in dealing with the significance of Henry VIII's religious innovations. The topic can still elicit sprightly discussions among them.

A visitor to England can feel close to Henry VIII by visiting Hampton Court Palace, just outside of London. Magnificent in Tudor brick and sprouting hundreds of chimneys, the palace was built by his right-hand man, Cardinal Wolsey. Hampton Court can be readily reached by a Green Line bus.

Henry's first wife, Catherine of Aragon, a serious Spanish queen, produced his daughter Mary, who later ruled as Mary I, or "Bloody Mary." Henry's great passion for Anne Boleyn was one of the most remarkable romances of all history. Because of Henry's unbounded passion for her, he divorced Catherine of Aragon and made Anne queen. Love soon turned to hate, however, and Anne was executed, leaving a daughter, who would become Elizabeth I. Henry's next wife, Jane Seymour, died in childbirth, but the child was the long-awaited male heir, who became Edward VI. Henry had no other children by his other wives, Catherine Howard, Anne of Cleves and Catherine Parr. The fate of these ladies can be recalled by the schoolboy's rhyme: "Divorced, beheaded, died; divorced, beheaded, survived." They made up a total of three Catherines, two Annes, and one Jane.

After Henry VIII died in 1547, he was succeeded by his only son, Edward VI, who was still a child, and a sickly one at that. He died at sixteen after being a manipulated child king for only six years. Henry VIII's two daughters followed, eldest first. Mary I was a tragic figure, a pious Roman Catholic like her mother, a woman who had to put her religious principles above prudence and all else. She became notorious for burning Protestants at the stake at the notorious "Smithfield Fires." Outside of her religious fanaticism, Mary was the kindest of the Tudors, but she has gone down in history as "Bloody Mary." She is sometimes confused with Mary, Queen of Scots, who was also Catholic, but a member of the Stuart family instead of the Tudor dynasty. Mary, Queen of Scots, played a role in the reign of Elizabeth.

The Elizabethan Age, 1558-1603

Most Americans are familiar to some degree with Elizabeth I. Her reign marked the blossoming of the Renaissance in England and the nation's first efforts at colonization in the New World. She was Henry VIII's second daughter. Her mother was the lively Anne Boleyn, who was beheaded not long after Elizabeth's birth. She succeeded her half-sister, Mary I, and ruled thereafter for a colorful and dramatic half century, from 1558 to 1603. This was truly a golden age: a time of spiritual, cultural and economic expansion and achievement. Shakespeare is the most famous of many, many creative Elizabethans.

Like other golden ages, it was also a time of immense international tension, as the Catholic Counter-Reformation gained strength on the continent. English sea dogs, who were really semi-pirates, found adventure on all the oceans, particularly against the Spanish. Assassination was a constant threat for Elizabeth. Mary, the flamboyant, emotional and highly attractive Queen of Scots, was the Catholic heir to Elizabeth's throne who waited in the wings. Finally, Mary was beheaded because she was implicated in plots against Elizabeth.

Tudor Architecture

Tudor architecture was unique, and fortunately much of it has been preserved. In later centuries, it continued to inspire English and American architects, to the extent that today Tudor style — black and white pseudo timbering — can be seen in townhouse developments being built in such places as Colorado.

Although expensive, bricks were esteemed by the Tudor architects who built the great mansions of the era. Elaborate brickwork patterns and numerous and highly decorated chimneys were characteristic of their handiwork. Less imposing structures, such as inns, farmhouses and merchants' houses, were frequently made of "half timber." These buildings are striking because the timber was usually painted black, and framed by white plaster and lath panels. A "zebra effect" was often achieved. All of the very old towns of

Britain have at least some of these treasured Tudor originals. Unfortunately, the Great Fire of London in 1666 and the many great fires in World War II claimed all too many of these highly combustible buildings.

Interestingly, at least some Americans do not like the black and white pattern, complaining that the stark contrasts are too glaring for their eyes. For most Americans, however, these Tudor half-timber buildings are ineffably charming.

In Tudor times, architecture again reveals something of history. The buildings are transitional, just as the times were transitional from medieval to modern. The great houses of the nobility are no longer castles because castles can no longer hold out against artillery. Architecture, therefore, shows that the great nobles could no longer resist the Tudor crown. Even so, the gate houses and the teeth-like tops of turrets, called crenellation, are decorations reminiscent of the castles of the Middle Ages.

THE STUART ERA 1603-1714

Chronology of the Seventeenth Century

It is fairly easy to arrange the Stuart era chronologically. It covers roughly the seventeenth century, and the kings can be remembered by this string of letters: J-C-O-C-J, for the reigns of James I (1603-1625); Charles I (1625-1649); Charles II (1660-1685); and James II (1685-1688). Remember that the J's are on the outside and the C's are on the inside and that two I's come first, followed by two II's. The "O" in the middle stands for Oliver Cromwell, who ruled most of the time during the interregnum, or times without kings, which lasted from 1649 until the Restoration of 1660. During the interregnum, there were two republican forms of government, called the "commonwealth" and the "protectorate." In actuality, both were dependent upon Cromwell's military power.

The Civil Wars and the Gentry

The central dramatic event in Stuart history was the English Civil War, the time when royalists, called Cavaliers, fought on the side of the king and Parliamentarians, called Roundheads because of their helmets, fought against the king. These struggles, from 1642-1648, were colorful and romantic, but they also had much to do with important changes in English society. The rise of capitalism and the rise of radical Protestant religion (Puritanism) had much to do with their origin. So did the ineffective rule of the first two Stuart kings.

James I, for whom the King James version of the Bible is named, was a pretentious Scot. The term Jacobean refers to the period of his reign because it is derived from the Hebrew name for James, which is Jacob. His reign saw the first permanent English settlement in America, in Jamestown in 1607. Charles I, although he was often incompetent and irresolute and devious, strove for absolutism in England, something that went against the grain of the long tradition of Parliamentary government and common law.

The group that presented the most forceful and effective opposition to the Stuart kings came from a class unique to England and highly represented in the House of Commons — the gentry. These were the proud, well-educated, active and public-spirited landowners who were just below the aristocracy and, therefore, non-noble, although they did have coats of arms. As a group, they descended from the medieval knights, were called "Sir" and usually had "Esquire" tacked to the ends of their names. Great Virginia families, such as the Madison or Washington families, lived lives that were similar to those of the English gentry.

In the early seventeenth century, significant numbers of the gentry became radicals in religion as Puritans and revolutionaries against the crown. From their bastion of power in the House of Commons, they were able to break the power of the Stuart kings and limit the power of the British monarchy for all time to come. Thereafter, the gentry turned away from revolutionary excesses and became rather conservative. They held power on the land and in local government all over England, and they dominated the House of Commons as well. Their hold on British politics lasted until the nineteenth century, and even today their influence in Britain is far from negligible.

Oliver Cromwell and Puritanism, 1649-1660

Once Charles I was beheaded by a so-called "Rump Parliament," consisting of the radical members, a remarkable and formerly rather obscure Puritan country gentleman, Oliver Cromwell, took over the state. Although he sought to rule with Parliament, the times were so chaotic that for the first and only time in English history, a virtual military dictatorship prevailed. Revolution had ended in arbitrary rule by a general. Ever after, militarism has had a bad reputation in Britain. Ever since, except during the World Wars, British standing armies have been small, professional and nonpolitical.

Religious fanaticism was another aspect of the period between royal reigns (1649-1660), called the interregnum, which gained widespread disrepute. All sorts of raving fanatics came out of the shadows, and sects multiplied with amazing speed. Some were so radical in social behavior that Cromwell's soldiers had to suppress them. Since Puritanism, which can be considered a general tendency towards simpler or more extreme Protestantism, was tied to Cromwell and the revolution, it also fell into disrepute as military rule became more and more distasteful. Therefore, after Cromwell died, the Puritans found themselves a despised minority in England.

Many English Puritans gave up on their home country and left for America, where the strong legacy of Puritanism can still be found, particularly in New England. American Presbyterians, Baptists, Congregationalists and a number of independent denominations can all trace their origins back to England during the Puritan revolution. Their emphasis on sermons, simplicity and the Bible indicates the Puritan heritage.

Many of the defeated and despised English Puritans stayed on in old England, where they were tolerated and called "Nonconformists" or "Dissenters" because they did not conform to the reestablished Anglican Church. Toleration of them did not mean, however, that they were free from discrimination. Toleration merely meant that they were allowed to believe whatever they wanted to without persecution. Social and political discrimination against them lasted for over a century, during which time many of the Nonconformists turned to making fortunes in business and industry.

Cromwell himself has gone down in history as

both a hero and a villain. It is difficult to be impartial about this important figure in British history. To Catholics, particularly Irish Roman Catholics, he was a scourge, but to Baptists, Presbyterians or Congregationalists, he was a knight in shining armor.

The Restoration of 1660 and the Glorious Revolution of 1688

For Americans, it seems curious that a republic was replaced with a restored monarchy in 1660. The Stuarts came back to the throne in large measure because royal governance was normal for seventeenth century society and because Charles II promised to be a limited and constitutional monarch who would obey the laws of the realm and guarantee all Englishmen their freedoms. Another reason for the Restoration was that the gentry had been soured against radical experimentation in church and state by the excesses of the interregnum. This powerful landed class was, therefore, quite willing to welcome back a Stuart monarch and reestablish the Anglican Church along with the monarchy.

Charles II turned out to be a kindly, skillful, genial lecher devoted to getting as much pleasure out of life as possible. James II succeeded him, and constitutional troubles came to the fore again. James II, a Roman Catholic, tried to fill offices in the state and army with his co-religionists, and suspended laws which were designed to keep the government of England in Protestant control. His activities backfired; the landed classes overthrew him and invited his Protestant daughter, Mary, to reign along with her Dutch husband, William of Orange. This *coup d'etat* was the much celebrated "Glorious Revolution" of 1688, which came to reaffirm the limited nature of the English monarchy. It demonstrated the principle that monarchs who broke their contracts could be fired. Americans subsequently made use of this point, and they also adopted almost all of the Bill of Rights that was promulgated immediately after the Glorious Revolution. This document is fundamental to the constitution of both countries and demonstrates why both countries are so similar when it comes to dealing with important rights, liberties and freedoms.

The Last Stuarts and the Wars with France

William and Mary were followed by another of James II's Protestant daughters, Queen Anne (1702-1714). Anne had the sad distinction of begetting seventeen children, all of whom died.

From the time of the Glorious Revolution onward, it was clear that powerful France, dominant on the Continent, had become a national enemy much as Spain had been in the sixteenth century. As Britain arranged coalitions of Continental states to fight French expansion, the Churchill family rose to prominence. John Churchill, Winston Churchill's ancestor, became the first Duke of Marlborough for winning military glory against the French on the Continent.

Cultural Achievements in the Later Stuart Period

English literature and theatre maintained a high reputation for creativity and richness in this period. In architecture, the genius of Christopher Wren was at work. Not only did he design St. Paul's Cathedral and dozens of churches, he also supervised the rebuilding of London after the disastrous Great Fire of 1666, which left most of the older parts of London a smoldering ruin. Christopher Wren employed classical features, such as domes and columns, on structures which were strongly influenced by the Renaissance in France and Italy. This Renaissance impulse sought to incorporate the restraint, discipline and order of ancient times in a graceful, moderate style.

Some of the greatest achievements in British science belong to the latter seventeenth century, perhaps in part attributable to the inclination of many talented people to turn away from the vexed topics of religion and spend their energies on the exploration of the natural world. The giant among these scientists was Sir Isaac Newton, whose world view of physics lasted until the time of Einstein, and which still has many practical applications today. Newton shares with Charles Darwin the distinction of being one of the two greatest British scientists of all time.

THE GEORGIAN ERA, 1714-1789

The Dominance of the Landed Classes

This period takes its name from the four Georges who ruled England, I, II, III and IV, in that order. The last George in this series died in 1830, but the eruption of the French Revolution in 1789 can be used to mark the coming of a new era. In addition, the industrial revolution beginning to get underway by the 1770s would transform Britain for all time. Therefore, there is some logic in ending the Georgian period in 1789.

For the last time in British history, the landed classes — the aristocracy and the gentry — clearly dominated society and politics. By the next century, the middle class was to grow in number and importance to the extent that it could seek to wrest control from the landed classes, but in the eighteenth century the power and style of the aristocracy and gentry prevailed without challenge.

These four Georges were called Hanoverians because their dynasty came from the small German province of that name. They were the closest Protestant heirs to the English throne, for a law passed in the early eighteenth century disqualified Roman Catholics from the throne. Therefore, the Stuart line, exiled in France, was disqualified even through their lineage was more royal than that of these Germans. Since the first two of these Georges were foreign, homesick and rather limited intellectually, great English statesmen who sat in the House of Commons and the House of Lords took over much of the function of the executive branch of government. They passed out honors in the king's name, arranged for appointments to ministries and jockeyed among themselves for political prominence.

The organs of government that evolved because the Hanoverians were weak monarchs are highly significant for the development of the British Constitution. In a quiet, generally informal manner, the British politicians of Georgian England worked out the practice of cabinet government. Operating together, a small group of key ministers formed the first cabinets, and the most important of them gained the title of Prime Minister, ironically a term of derision at first. Almost invariably, all of these politicians had to command substantial followings in the legislature to be at the center of things.

The first of the Prime Ministers was Sir Robert

Walpole, a skilled manipulator of patronage and influence. Later in the century, two Prime Ministers named Pitt, father and son, gained fame. William Pitt the Elder was a great war leader who was in charge during the French and Indian War, which is usually called the Seven Years' War in Europe. Pittsburgh, Pennsylvania, was named after him. He was sympathetic to the American cause in the era of the American Revolution. William Pitt the Elder became the Earl of Chatham late in life and is therefore sometimes known as Chatham. His son, William Pitt the Younger, picked up the pieces for King George III after the American Revolution and continued in office until he died while the wars with Napoleon were still going on. William Pitt the Younger became Prime Minister in his early twenties.

Georgian Architecture, Art and Style

Georgian England's architecture clearly reveals how the landed classes dominated society. Most of the great families had their "big house," or mansion, or seat, in the countryside. These were often great and gorgeous structures. Nowadays, many of them have been taken over by the National Trust so that these places can be "stately homes" open to tourists. In addition, Georgian aristocrats and gentry owned "town houses," a term that did not have the current American meaning of undetached row housing. The Georgian town houses were large, substantial, expensive places, usually grouped around squares in London. Today, most of them are divided up for use as hotels and expensive flats, but at least some of their grandeur remains. The town house was used during the social and political season, when life in the country was the most drab. In addition, the landed classes were likely to go to a spa for part of the year. Bath was particularly popular, as its great crescents of Georgian buildings testify.

The great buildings of Georgian England tell much about the spirit of the times. The grandest palace of them all, Blenheim, just outside Oxford, was built for the first Duke of Marlborough. The dozens of other palatial Georgian mansions were built for aristocrats and landed gentlemen as well, and not for the dull members of the royal family of the eighteenth century. On the Continent, monumental buildings were apt to be royal buildings.

The baroque and rococo styles were in full bloom on the Continent in the eighteenth century, the former powerful and the latter highly decorative. English baroque buildings tend to be rare. Neoclassical styles and buildings that were generally more restrained, proportioned and less highly ornamental were characteristic of England when compared to the Continent. Their interior decorations repeated classical motifs, drawing inspiration from ancient Greece and Rome. Usually light, delicate colors were used in the eighteenth century: gold, silver, light blue, pink, white and lavender. Jasmine Wedgwood china, popular in the United States, gives some indication of Georgian decoration.

Hard riding, hard drinking English aristocracy and landed gentry fancied themselves the new Romans of the world, and their classical education reinforced this view. Restraint, discipline, proportion and moderation were supposed to be their ideals. They were certainly self-assured and confident that God had placed them over millions of poor and toiling agricultural laborers, whom they paid a pittance to work on their huge estates. This exploitation of the poor by the rich should also be kept in mind when viewing these great houses.

Life for the Other Classes

No matter how grandly they lived, the upper, landed classes were comparatively small in number. Eighteenth century Britain had another vital sector of life in the growing but not yet dominant middle classes. The "shopocracy," as they were called, vigorously plied their trades in all Britain's cities. The London of Dr. Johnson and his biographer Boswell reached out to the world of trade as no other city anywhere. Countless merchants, bankers, insurance agents and retailers enriched themselves as that lengthy development called the rise of the middle classes continued to unfold.

Below the middle class were the masses. They often experienced cruelty, wretchedness and misery, whether they lived in urban or rural environments. England in the eighteenth century was similar to parts of Asia or Africa today, where the very rich and the very poor live in close physical proximity, but are miles apart in lifestyles. Debtors' prisons, infanticide, widespread crime, an epidemic of alcoholism from cheap gin, widespread venereal disease and chronic malnutrition blighted the lives of the British poor in the eighteenth century.

Misery had always been the lot of the submerged masses of the world, but what made the eighteenth century different was an incipient humanitarian movement that expressed a new social criticism and made efforts to provide remedies. Many hospitals and various charitable organizations originated in this century.

In religion, the most notable development was Methodism. It was an offshoot of the established Anglican Church which Methodism's founder, John Wesley, found too cold, distant, unemotional and impersonal for the needs of ordinary people. Wesley began to preach outdoors to the poor, sending a warm message that stressed personal salvation.

BRITAIN IN AN AGE OF REVOLUTION

The Era of the French Revolution, Napoleon and Romanticism: 1789-1815

Since the American Revolution is a very special topic that bears directly on Anglo-American relations, it appears in the chapter on politics, under Sensitive Areas.

The years of the French Revolution and Napoleon were exciting and heroic, as great monuments all over Britain commemorating events in this era attest. For a time, Britain faced invasion alone, as the nation would against the Nazis. Her historic enemy, France, under a new, revolutionary ideology that was thrust forth by the bayonets of Napoleon, posed a threat to the British way of life. Two great heroes emerged to stop the French. Horatio Nelson, one-armed, one-eyed and five feet tall, stopped the French at Trafalgar in 1805 and died at the battle's close. The Duke of Wellington stopped Napoleon's forces at Waterloo in 1815.

Times of tension and change in history often bring on a burst of cultural creativity. In this era, the great romantic poets and writers flourished: Keats,

Shelley, Wordsworth, Coleridge and Sir Walter Scott. Romanticism stressed the overwhelming forces of nature, religion and emotion. It celebrated the glories of the Middle Ages and distant exotic cultures. Romanticism left its impress upon architecture, art and music in addition to literature, as classical restraints and proportion were broken through by a surge of feelings.

The Era of the Industrial Revolution, 1770-1840

The Industrial Revolution is extremely significant in British history because the very first appearance of this phenomenon, which has since swept the world, was in Britain. All subsequent industrializations, whether they took place in Germany, the Soviet Union or Korea, have copied to some extent the techniques and methods pioneered first in Britain. Britain's leap into industrial production came from a spontaneous breakthrough, and there are several good reasons why it came to Britain first. There was an extensive preexisting worldwide network of capitalistic trade, good resources in coal and iron ore, a spirit of inventiveness, a skilled workforce in carpentry and metal trades, an elaborate financial infrastructure, good transportation facilities, a government friendly to enterprise and much wealth to invest.

Between 1770 and 1840, industrialism in Britain took off and became airborne in permanent, self-sustaining growth and development. Changes came fast and were dramatic, massive and irreversible. Labor changed from hand to machine as power came from machines instead of muscles and wind; more and more consumer goods were produced by machine at generally decreasing cost per item; fortunes were made everywhere. All of this had a deep effect on the structure of British society. Industrialization led to rapid urban growth, the creation of an urban factory proletariat, and a broadening of the middle class strata. Rapidly growing cities needed more lawyers, doctors, teachers, bankers and managers. Eventually, Britain had the world's first society with an urban majority and the first society where the middle classes were so numerous and influential that they came to dominate much of politics and culture. This was a key feature underlying Victorian society.

For the generations undergoing these changes for the first time, the costs in human suffering were staggering, as the reader of Marx or Dickens knows. But once industrial production was well under way, widespread affluence and comfort were the results.

Britain still celebrates its special role in the Industrial Revolution. Museums display old machinery as treasures; huge railway museums exist; and places in the industrial northern part of England have been set aside to commemorate the origin of the factory system. Coalbrookdale and Ironbridge museums in Shropshire are exceptional in this regard. It was in this northern part of England, in Lancashire and the western portion of Yorkshire in particular, that the factory system got underway. Visitors can still see grim streets and buildings that go back to this era in such places as Bradford, Leeds, Rochdale, Manchester and Liverpool. But tourists rarely go to these cities, often called "black England." Tourists are apt to stay in the warmer south, called "green England," places where early heavy industry did not get its start because coal and iron deposits were not to be found there.

A psychological inheritance from this era exists as well. For roughly a century, Britain led the whole world in technology. Things were produced faster, better and with a higher technology than anywhere else in the world. By contrast, American industrial development was in its early stages in the North, and through most of the nineteenth century in general America was regarded as a vast agrarian area noted for producing raw materials and foodstuffs. American food, cotton and timber were exchanged for the wonderful cheap goods from Britain's booming factories. In the present age, when the United States, Japan and West Germany all lead Britain in most (but not all) advances in what we call "high tech" industry, the previous span of British superiority is remembered with remorse mixed with pride.

THE EARLY NINETEENTH CENTURY

The Regency Era: 1811-1830

The Regency era began in 1811, the year that the future King George IV came to rule in place of George III, who became mentally incapacitated, or, as he was described then, "sad and mad." The term Regency comes from the title of "Prince Regent" that the future George IV took until his father died in 1820. The Regency era continued to 1830, when George IV himself died.

In art and architecture, Regency style was powerful. Buildings tended to be massive and neoclassical, meaning that regularity, order and discipline were imposed. Greek and Roman motifs, such as *bas reliefs* and Doric columns, prevailed. Many imposing structures in London date from this era, especially along Regent's Street, in the Trafalgar Square area and near Regent's Park.

The Era of the Reform Bill, 1830-1837

For Europe in general, the early nineteenth century was a revolutionary era, as impulses from the French revolution toward equality convulsed Europe in waves of upheavals which occurred in 1820, 1830 and 1848. Britain was singularly unique in avoiding revolution. Why was this so? The answer is complex, but it can be said that gradualism and compromise operated within a deeply rooted and somewhat representative Parliamentary system to the extent that a Reform Bill satisfied enough people so that revolution was avoided.

The British Parliament actually passed a series of Reform Bills in 1832, 1867 and 1884. But the first of these was the greatest because it pointed the way to the gradual achievement of democracy in the future. What it did was to broaden the franchise by giving the vote to the newly emerging middle classes; create new electoral districts for the new industrial centers; and eliminate small and corrupt electoral districts called "rotten" or "pocket" boroughs from which the landed classes had drawn much of their political power. The bill did not go far enough for the British working classes, who had agitated for democracy. Even so, the Reform Bill of 1832 marked the successful inclusion of the new industrial society into the operation of the British Constitution. Evolution, not revolution, was to be the British mode of change.

By contrast, on the Continent middle class types were apt to be ardent revolutionaries, at least up until 1848. In Britain, the middle classes came to believe that their limited, constitutional monarchy was moving towards greater and greater liberalism. Hence, they supported the system against any would-be revolutionaries. The Reform Bill of 1832 guaranteed that the last revolution in British history remained that of 1688.

THE MAGNIFICENT VICTORIAN ERA, 1837-1901

The Spirit of the Times

The long reign of Queen Victoria, 1837-1901, has left its undeniable stamp on the Britain of today, materially and psychologically. It was the time of Britain's apogee, or high point, when Britain led the world in science, technology, politics, power and influence. Never before and never since the Victorian era has Britain been so important to the whole world. Britain's role in the nineteenth century was similar in many ways to the American role after World War II, except that Britain did not have an international rivalry as the one the United States has had with the Soviet Union. *Pax Britannica,* or the peace of Britain, was imposed and usually welcomed on all of the oceans of the globe by the unchallenged British navy.

Progress was the all-important word for the Victorian era. Victorians believed in it, and saw themselves as the most progressive people in the world, as they witnessed invention following invention and science advancing on a broad front to control nature for the apparent benefit of humankind. Victorians could measure progress in so many tangible ways: production was dramatically up in coal, iron, textiles, shipbuilding and in a wide range of consumer goods. Railroads transformed the landscape, and everywhere efficiency and speed came to be taken as British hallmarks. Victorians could also measure progress in political changes. As the century unfolded, more and more people got the right to vote as the government gradually became more liberal and responsive. Old bastions of privilege and discrimination were removed one by one in a free Parliament where reason, discussion, debate and voting determined decisions.

Victorians were free from many worries of the twentieth century. Pollution was not as serious a concern as today; science did not appear as a dangerous genie, and modern totalitarianism, either fascism or communism, had not yet emerged. It was a time when Britain had the most admired political system in the world, along with dramatically improving lifestyles, and the whole world seemed to be maturing in Britain's direction.

The Victorians exhibited unique psychological characteristics that directly influenced American grandmothers and may continue to influence us all indirectly today. Ideally, Victorians were strict in their morality, pious and committed to the work ethic. Thrift, discipline, honesty, temperance, hard work, earnestness, obedience to God's Word and cleanliness were all celebrated Victorian virtues. Sex was only to be expressed in marriage and repressed otherwise. While characteristic contemporary life for many Americans has departed far from Victorian virtues, it can be argued that the prevalence of guilt feelings, the penchant for cleanliness and the phenomenon of the workaholic indicate that the Victorian inheritance is still with us psychologically.

Some Victorian Achievements

Famous Victorians are legion. This was the world of Charles Dickens, Rudyard Kipling, Thomas Hardy,

Keats, Shelley, Sir Walter Scott and Alfred, Lord Tennyson, to name but a few in literature. It was the world of Gilbert and Sullivan on stage. In politics, two great figures dominated the later years of Victoria's reign: Benjamin Disraeli, a novelist of Jewish background, and William Gladstone, the embodiment of open-minded liberalism and pious leadership. In foreign policy, the irascible and dashing Lord Palmerston celebrated and fostered British interests throughout the world.

The British Empire grew in all directions in Victoria's heyday, stretching over "palm and pine." "The sun never sets on the British Empire" was a true cliché in Victorian times. It meant that the sun had to be shining on some part of it somewhere on the globe during all 24 hours. Eventually, one-fourth of the earth's surface and one-fourth of its people came to live under the Union Jack, a remarkable achievement for such a small island. Beyond this, there was an informal empire of trade, wherein British goods, ships, money and services operated profitably almost everywhere.

The Victorians were great builders, inventors, developers and producers since they were the first people who harnessed machines to their economy. Goods of all sorts from the Victorian era can be found everywhere in Britain today as well as in many other parts of the world. Much of this unbelievable clutter of furniture and mass-produced products goes under the rubric of "antiques" today. In addition, there are acres of Victorian buildings, great Victorian bridges and aqueducts, and an essentially Victorian railway system.

Victorian Arts

Victorians did not produce great visual arts by anyone's standards, but today younger people tend to appreciate the "charm" of Victoriana more than many older people who had to grow up with it in their parents' or grandparents' homes. Furniture was overstuffed. There was too much clutter and too much sentimental coyness. Nonfunctional decoration ran riot. Perhaps the most familiar example of it known to Americans is in the form of "gingerbread" decoration on buildings. But all kinds of structures, even structures as functional as railway bridges, received typical Victorian superfluous decoration.

The Victorians really had no true style of their own. Instead, their arts were what is called eclectic, meaning that they borrowed from here and there. The Middle Ages provided their favorite source of inspiration, and this reveals the Victorians' essential romanticism. The medieval castles, cathedrals and knights in shining armor were highly romantic in the eyes of Victorians, and they celebrated the medieval world in their literature and arts.

Victorian appreciation for the medieval era has served to disadvantage the American visitor. Many seemingly medieval creations turn out to be just over a hundred years old. So the visitor may go into a grim, brooding, turreted hulk of an Anglican church building in suburban London and think it the very essence of a medieval setting — until he or she discovers that the Victorians erected it in the 1880s.

A Victorian Paradox: Romanticism and Materialism

A striking contradiction of the Victorians is that

they were so romantic in the midst of such intense material preoccupations. They were obsessed with making things and making money from their efforts. The Victorian world of business was a hard world of facts, figures and balances. Yet at the same time their paintings celebrate sentimental dogs and children, medieval heroes and imaginative fairies. Their authors, many of whom are still avidly read today, used comparable themes. The romanticism of Victorian art and literature seems to have functioned as an escape, or a change of pace, from the harsh, practical and prosaic realities Victorians faced.

Contemporary Americans still curl up with Sherlock Holmes or a Dickens novel and transport themselves back to foggy nights in Victorian London. The fogs are no longer there, thanks to strict air ordinances, but American visitors can find rich deposits of Victoriana everywhere. When we come to think of it, contemporary Americans might have something of their own version of the Victorian paradox: the nation that builds so many interstate highways, minicomputers, cars and aircraft carriers is also responsible for the world of Walt Disney, E.T. and Star Wars.

THE EDWARDIAN ERA, 1901-1914

Although the king for whom the era is named died in 1910, the Edwardian era is generally regarded as the period from 1901, the year Victoria died, to 1914, the year that World War I broke out.

Impressions of the quality of life in Britain during this time span vary considerably. The wealthy and well born usually remember the Edwardian era as a glorious sunset on a world where the Empire, capitalism, social life and British influence throughout the world were all splendid. The humbly born might recall the huge disparities between rich and poor, the long hours of work for low pay, the slums and the lack of all but the beginnings of welfare provisions. All might agree that it was a brassier, more strident age than the Victorian era. The popular song of the times, "Ta-Ra-Ra-Boom-De-Ay," captures something of its essence.

The Edwardian era began at the conclusion of a nasty little imperialistic war in South Africa, the Boer War, which the British won at considerable cost. The war revealed the widespread unpopularity of the British in Europe. The Afrikaners, the Dutch descendants who had lived in South Africa since the seventeenth century, had the sympathy of the Europeans because they appeared to be the underdogs heroically resisting very aggressive British imperialism led by Cecil Rhodes, a diamond magnate. The British made matters worse by terminating Afrikaner guerilla resistance by means of a scorched earth policy and the use of concentration camps. British recognition of hostility and their isolation in Europe led to attempts to form *ententes,* or mild alliances, with European powers thereafter. This, in turn, helped bring Britain into World War I.

No matter how high the status of British capitalism in the Edwardian era, the period also marked the beginnings of the modern welfare state. Old age pensions and national health insurance were inaugurated during this time. Britain was behind Germany and other European states in this, but far ahead of the United States.

Socialist theory also made headway in the Edwardian period. One very characteristically British kind of

socialism was that of the Fabian Socialists, who included George Bernard Shaw and Sidney and Beatrice
Webb in their membership. The former was the
greatest English playwright since Shakespeare, and the
latter were a team of social scientists whose works are
still important. The Fabian Socialists were intellectuals
who sought to convince influential people of the rational and just nature of socialism brought about by
democratic means. At first, they worked to prove the
practical nature of socialism at the local level by taking
over such things as gas and water services, which gave
them the nickname "gas and water socialists."

About the same time, masses of unskilled workers
enrolled in large, militant unions. These unions and
several groups of socialists came together in the
Edwardian era to form the Labour Party. While it was
only a minor party in the period before World War I,
its influence, as well as the influence of the Fabians,
would come to the fore later, particularly after World
War II.

In all of this, Marxists played a very small role. In
general, British Labour politics did not accept the
Marxist view of the inevitability of class warfare.

Another movement of the Edwardian era that was
to have a major bearing upon the future was the Suf-
fragette Movement aimed at gaining votes for women.
The right to vote was viewed as the key to ending
male dominance and discrimination in many fields.
The more militant suffragettes deliberately broke the
law by doing highly visible and outrageous deeds, such
as setting fires and destroying private property, in order to draw attention to their movement.

Yet another source of tension was Ireland, where
home rule was destined to occur. A major act had
passed Parliament in 1911 which severely limited the

power of the House of Lords. Henceforth, this ancient body could only delay legislation somewhat. It could no longer block legislation the way the United States Senate can. For Ireland, this meant that self-rule would be passed. Nevertheless, in Ulster militant Protestants declared that they would fight rather than be dominated by a Roman Catholic majority ruling from Dublin. Then as now, the British were faced with a seemingly insoluble Irish situation. Civil war loomed. The only thing that prevented it was the outbreak of World War I. Protestant and Catholic Irish energies poured into the war effort. So did the efforts of militant union members and militant suffragettes. World War I absorbed whole currents of tension and potential violence stemming from Edwardian times in its own great violence.

For the rich who were not interested in women's rights, socialism, poverty, or Ireland, the Edwardian era could be delightful. The monarch, Edward VII, personified so much of the tastes of the rich in his time. Queen Victoria's eldest son had always been something of a hedonist and Francophile, at odds with his strict and Germanophile upbringing. Wine, women, song and gargantuan, spectacular consumption were the hallmarks of the upper class that followed Edward's example. The style parallels the Gilded Age in America, resplendent in the conspicuous consumption of people like the Vanderbilts.

THE ERA OF WORLD WAR I

Contrasts with the American Experience in the War

The joys of Edwardian Britain came to an abrupt

end with the outbreak of World War I in the summer of 1914. Britain and Europe were never the same again, as deep trauma settled upon civilization. Americans seldom appreciate the depth of the impact of this tragic war upon Europe. Perhaps this is because American participation was nothing on the scale of British participation. The United States entered the war late, in 1917, and most of the United States' forces never got to the front lines. While America suffered with 50,000 deaths, Britain endured 750,000 deaths. In fact, Britain lost twice as many of its people in World War I than in World War II, a longer contest, 1939 to 1945, which featured heavy bombing of civilian areas from the air.

In addition to all of those who were killed or wounded, and all of those who lost husbands, fathers, sons, brothers, sweethearts and potential mates, the war brought psychological ramifications that are extremely strong and complex, and included such phenomena as individuals' alienation from Western civilization and disgust at what was formerly held in high esteem, such as nationalism. On the Continent, the war led to a new, sick nationalism, called fascism. Perhaps one way for Americans to come to grips with the impact of World War I on Europe is contemplate the varied reactions and difficulties expressed by returning Vietnam veterans. Interesting parallels can be drawn between them and the returning survivors of World War I.

Causes of the War

In Britain, one frequently hears the name "the First German War" for World War I, and, indeed, many still choose to blame the war upon the Kaiser and German militarism. Yet historians have shown that all of the major participants and some of the minor ones were to a degree guilty and to a degree innocent regarding the outbreak of the war. Seen this way, the ruthless sacrifice of the blood and treasure of European civilization from 1914 to 1918 was simply a tragedy on a monumental scale.

When the Archduke Franz Ferdinand of Austria-Hungary was assassinated by a Serbian nationalist, a diplomatic crisis ensued. To British people, the situation seemed just one more crisis in a long series of Balkan troubles. They were as used to them as contemporary Americans are used to Middle Eastern crises. Unfortunately, this particular Balkan crisis got out of hand and escalated into a small war between Austria and Serbia. This in turn escalated into a world war as the major powers lined up to support their allies.

Britain had an *entente*, or loose alliance, with France and Russia, two nations with whom Britain was able to smooth out imperial rivalries around the globe. Anglo-German amity was ruined by the headlong effort of the Germans to build a great fleet. The German fleet was a direct threat to Britain because the country imported a substantial amount of food and raw materials over the oceans. What decided British participation was the German invasion of Belgium, a country whose neutrality was guaranteed by Britain and several other powers. Belgium had a particular strategic significance for the British, since it was the logical place from which to launch an invasion of the British Isles.

British Participation in World War I

British participation in World War I was similar to

that of France and Germany in that it involved costly, dreadful campaigns that seemed to get nowhere. The western front consisted of a maze of trenches stretching from Switzerland's border across France and across Belgium to the sea. The British fought on the western part of the western front, in Belgium, for the most part. The most tragic losses "in Flanders' fields" came along the Somme River. Up to 60,000 British casualties were recorded there in a single day of fighting. Year after year, armies on both sides hurled masses of foot soldiers against barbed wire, machine guns and artillery without breaking the stalemate. Defensive weapons had the advantages. The offensive weapons of the next war — the plane and the tank — were in early and experimental stages during World War I.

Gallipoli was an ill-fated campaign that sought to open a way through to Russia via the Turkish-controlled Dardanelles. Winston Churchill, at the admiralty, was wrongfully blamed for the costly British failure at Gallipoli.

At sea, there was only one major battle on the surface, Jutland, which was something of a draw. The much feared German fleet stayed in port thereafter. The submarine fleet kept active, however, and mounted a very serious threat to the British war effort by threatening to cut off vital supplies. Convoy tactics eventually turned the tide.

The Winston Churchill of World War I was David Lloyd George, a Welshman who rose from obscurity to become a leading Liberal minister in the Edwardian era. When the war began, he displayed his ability by meeting the challenge of a munitions shortage. Thereafter, he engineered his acquisition of the office of Prime Minister. David Lloyd George was a dynamo of a leader, and a magnificent orator. He certainly had the will to victory. Yet he had a negative side as well, and remains a controversial figure. He was a ruthless politician.

Britain did win a few clear victories on the periphery of the main effort of the war. Palestine was wrested away from the Ottoman Turks, and the Germans were defeated in Africa. But the war was finally decided by attrition on the western front. Russia dropped out of the war the same year that the United States came into it, putting the whole focus on fighting in France and Belgium. After coming close to winning in a last surge in 1918, the Germans called for an armistice and the war was over.

THE INTERWAR ERA, 1918-1939

After the ferocious destruction of World War One, there was an attempt to get back to normal times. But the Edwardian assurance and opulence did not return for Britain in general. The image of the interwar era is that of being gray, grim and depressed. Unemployment was high throughout nearly the whole era, with some families living on the "dole" or welfare payments, decade after decade. Britain's most notable but aged industries, shipbuilding, coal mining, steel and textiles, were hardest hit by chronic depression. Meanwhile, light industries, such as the manufacture of electrical appliances, developed considerably, providing British consumers with all sorts of new products including tinned (canned) goods and various synthetics. On the one hand, there was considerable material progress for many consumers, but on the other there was bare subsistence for the unemployed millions. One way to appreciate the more dismal aspects of the period is to read George Orwell's *The Road to Wigan Pier.*

The dominant political figure of the period was Stanley Baldwin, a solid, stolid, businesslike and rather dull Conservative. Sometimes the twenties and early thirties are called the "age of Baldwin." Labour mustered its first and rather brief governments in the interwar period as well. These were governments formed in coalition. Labour never had a clear-cut majority until after World War II. The first Labour Prime Minister was J. Ramsay McDonald, who is still disparaged by many Labourites today for having sold out to the establishment once he got into power. His defenders point to his need to compromise in the circumstances he faced.

The interwar period marked the beginning of the dissolution of the British Empire. Ireland was the first to go. A small but violent rebellion had occurred in 1916. The British overreacted to this "Easter Rebellion" by executing many of its leaders and thereby made the movement for Irish nationalism more extreme. Home rule would no longer be enough. An independent republic was now desired by Irishmen willing to fight a civil war to get it. Britain sought to repress them, sending in the hated "Black and Tans," a voluntary and mercenary paramilitary force. Eventually, Lloyd George signed a peace treaty in 1923 which granted sovereignty to all of Ireland except six counties of Ulster. The ongoing tragedy of Ireland today can be traced back to this settlement. (See the section on Ireland under Sensitive Areas in the chapter on politics.)

Royalty became the focus of romantic drama in the 1930s. George V died in 1936, after having reigned since 1910 as a dutiful and appreciated monarch. His son succeeded him as Edward VIII. He only lasted for less than a year because of a dramatic set of events that captured headlines in 1936. The king fell hopelessly in love with Wallis Simpson, a twice-divorced American. Given the standards of the time, she was scandalous, their liaison was scandalous, and his plan to marry her was even more scandalous. As a consequence, the king of England abdicated his throne so that he could, in his words, marry the woman he loved. Thereafter he became an exile, with the title Duke of Windsor, and Mrs. Simpson became his duchess. Together they dedicated their lives to frivolous social life in various elegant places abroad. Edward's brother came to reign in his place from 1936 to 1952 as George VI. He was the father of Queen Elizabeth II.

Britain had its equivalent of America's roaring twenties, complete with flappers and jazz, but the dominant notes of life in interwar Britain for all too many people were those of depression. Talking to old-timers about the interwar period is an interesting pastime. Their bitter memories of hard times after World War I serve to explain why the electorate was so willing to go along with the seemingly radical proposals offered by Labour candidates in the election right at the close of World War II.

Appeasement, 1934-1939

The shadow of World War I haunted the foreign policy of the interwar period. Britain and other nations made numerous attempts to achieve disarmament or at least prevent arms races. All of these efforts proved futile when the rise of fascist dictatorships in

Germany, Italy and several lesser countries produced regimes committed to extreme nationalism and militarism. Only armed force could block their chronic, endemic aggression, but before this lesson had been learned, Britain endured grave humiliations in foreign policy.

Prime Minister Neville Chamberlain, always impeccably dressed, conveyed the impression of being a most reasonable and sensible British gentleman. Since the Treaty of Versailles was in increasing discredit, Chamberlain believed that he could appease or soothe the grievances of Nazi Germany by making sensible, reasonable and timely concessions. This policy of appeasement reached its greatest intensity when the national sovereignty of Czechoslovakia was virtually surrendered to the bullying of Hitler at Munich in 1938.

When Nazi aggression continued, Chamberlain and his followers realized how futile appeasement had been as a policy in dealing with fascist dictators. Thereafter, the British government began to rearm as fast as possible, as diplomacy changed course in order to confront aggression with agreements to go to war if other states were violated. Britain therefore went to war in September, 1939, when Germany attacked Poland.

The word "appeasement" passed into English usage as a pejorative term, meaning giving in to aggression. Its original meaning had been much more neutral, betokening attempts at conciliation. One outstanding British politician had warned against appeasement all along. Events proved Winston Churchill right, and when the war against Germany floundered in 1939 and 1940, Churchill became Prime Minister for the first time in his life, at sixty-four, an age when most men look forward to retirement.

THE ERA OF WORLD WAR II, 1939-1945

Contrasts between American and British Recollections of World War II

After the Japanese attack on Pearl Harbor, December 7, 1941, brought the United States into the war, a flood of men and material from North America poured into Britain and then leapt across the English Channel in the D-Day invasion of June, 1944. Both in Europe and the Pacific, the United States was clearly the dominant partner in the Anglo-American alliance. Therefore, it is natural that British memories of the Second World War should stress those aspects in which Britain fought alone, rather than when Britain functioned as a junior partner in the Anglo-American Alliance. These aspects include Dunkirk, the Battle of Britain, North Africa and Burma.

Interesting cultural exchanges took place between the millions of Americans who came to Britain in uniform and their British hosts. Many marriages resulted, and there was also some generally friendly rivalry. Americans always complained about the beer being warm. One Briton, exasperated at the deluge of Americans, made the famous declaration that American troops were "overpaid, oversexed and over here." The famous American response was that Britons were "underpaid, undersexed and under Eisenhower!"

Dunkirk

In 1940, the British army on the continent of Europe was rescued by a vast and varied flotilla of ships hastily thrown together and sent to the port of Dunkirk in France. When France was overwhelmed, the British army had retreated to this port. Although the British troops came home defeated and without their heavy equipment, Dunkirk was nevertheless seen as a great and heroic event. British soldiers faced adversity and overwhelming forces with stoic heroism, and were rescued by their fellow countrymen who risked their lives at sea on their behalf. The heroic retreat has always been a favorite motif of British nationalism; Dunkirk filled the bill admirably.

The Battle of Britain, June to September, 1940

Britain stood alone against the ferocious and undefeated might of Nazi Germany during the summer of 1940. While France was defeated, Russia continued to collaborate with Germany at this stage of the war. All of the other states of Europe were either conquered, frightened neutrals or German allies. The United States was not to enter the war until the end of 1941, so Britain and her far-flung dominions were the only forces in the whole world fighting against Nazi tyranny.

The Battle of Britain was unique in that it was fought almost entirely in the air. The German *Luftwaffe*, or air force, had the task of destroying the RAF (Royal Air Force) in preparation of an invasion, whose planning name was Operation Sea Lion. In order to carry out this risky invasion, the Germans had to have dominance in the air, which would compensate for their naval inferiority. Eliminating the RAF was essential to the undefeated Nazis.

The task proved impossible. Armed with beautiful, powerful and swift Spitfires, as well as with the stolid Hurricanes, the RAF shot down more German planes than they themselves lost. Except for one desperate period, replacements of men and planes came along just quickly enough to keep the RAF on top.

During the Battle of Britain, Prime Minister Winston Churchill produced some of his finest war oratory, as he led his nation in steely defiance of the Nazis. He called that dangerous time in history the British people's "finest hour," and long has it been celebrated as such. He also paid tribute to that small group of RAF pilots who held the Nazis at bay when he declared that never before in history was "so much owed by so many to so few." Pride in these times and in what Churchill's oratory celebrated is very special for British people, and American visitors are well advised to show appropriate respect for the Battle of Britain.

One wonderful way to strike up a conversation with British people over fifty-five is to ask them what they remember of the Battle of Britain. Nearly everyone has at least one good tale to tell.

The Blitz

Once they had given up their plans to invade England, the Nazis sought to pound the country into submission or a negotiated peace by launching massive bombing raids on London. The *Luftwaffe* came over nearly every night, sending down a rain of death and destruction. London, however, was simply too huge to demolish from the air, given the limited payloads of

German bombers. Londoners themselves adjusted to the "Blitz" surprisingly well, inspiring the world with their good humor. Hundreds of thousands of them took to sleeping in the underground (subway) stations, where a vibrant community life often developed. Londoners who survived the Blitz usually have a fund of great stories to tell.

North Africa and Burma

Both the North African and Burmese campaigns receive fuller attention in Britain than in the United States. General Montgomery was the hero in North Africa, noted for stopping General Rommel at El Alamein in 1942. Lord Mountbatten was the supreme commander in Southeast Asia whose primary role was to protect India from the Japanese and eventually to clear them out of Burma. Lord Mountbatten's distinguished career was ended a few years ago by a terrorist's bomb in Ireland.

Montgomery has been controversial in history. Many claim that he was a brilliant general and others maintain that he was phlegmatic and would never fight a major battle unless he had overwhelming superiority in men and equipment. Montgomery's failing attempt to force a crossing of the Rhine in the Netherlands in 1944 is often held against him. Many critics, most of them Americans, have alleged that the materials lavished on Montgomery's campaign should have been allocated to General Patton because he might have then had a chance to reach Berlin before the Russians.

Despite such controversy, Montgomery, Patton and several other noted generals pulled together under Eisenhower to bring British and American forces to the heart of what was supposed to have been Hitler's thousand-year Reich. It was a time of great men doing great deeds for great principles.

THE POSTWAR ERA, 1945 TO THE PRESENT

Many of the concerns of postwar Britain are of such an ongoing nature that they have been taken up in the chapters on politics and economics. What follows here is a summation of the main phenomena of an historical nature.

The Quiet Revolution and the Age of Austerity

In between V-E Day, Victory in Europe Day, in May, 1945, and V-J Day, Victory over Japan Day in August, Winston Churchill and his Conservative Party were given the sack (fired) by the electorate despite his soaring reputation as a great war leader. This dramatic and unexpected defeat did not stem from any lack of gratitude for the way Churchill had resolutely prosecuted the war. It came instead from a realization by the majority that the Labour Party had a program for social improvement while the Conservatives' plans were extremely vague. Too many recalled the grim circumstances that greeted the veterans returning home after World War I. The electorate wanted a program designed to avoid such hardship.

Labour planned to inaugurate the welfare state by building up the public sector of the economy and by carefully regulating the private sector. Under the calm, unassuming and rather colorless Clement Attlee as Prime Minister, changes came so fast in the period between 1945 and 1950 that it was called the "Quiet Revolution." Numerous industries were nationalized — railroads, gas, electricity, airways, docking facilities, the mines, the iron industry and the steel industry. Extensive social services for health, housing and the less fortunate were set up or expanded.

All of this required an enormous investment. The British economy was exhausted from its wartime sacrifices, but nevertheless a period of continued "austerity," or hard times of scarcity, was imposed on the patriotic, generally cooperative population until the new economy could be shaped. This monumental effort of self-sacrifice was substantially aided by the generous Marshall Plan grant of the United States, a fact that has not been forgotten by many Britons.

The End of Empire and the Birth of the Commonwealth

The British Empire came apart after World War II. New Zealand, Australia and Canada, where transplanted Britons comprised the dominant ethnic stock, had already attained sovereignty and self-government. South Africa was also self-governing. After World War II, almost all of the so-called black, brown and yellow colonies asserted their independence from the mother country. The largest piece of the Empire to go was India, which became independent in 1947, an event involving much bloodshed between Moslem and Hindu before the new states of India and Pakistan were established out of what had been British India.

Some violence accompanied the coming of independence elsewhere. Kenya, in East Africa, had the Mau-Mau uprising. Malaya was the scene of a vigorous spate of British counter-insurgency effort. Britain also

joined France and Israel to try to regain control of the
Suez Canal. America did not cooperate in the Suez
Crisis of 1956, and without U.S. backing, this attempt
to renew British influence in the Middle East col-
lapsed.

Despite these examples of conflict, the dismantling
of the largest empire that the world had ever seen
generally involved a peaceful transition to independence. The British had the good sense to realize that
the days of a colonial empire were over, and that it
was time to surrender power before it would be seized
from them by their former subjects. By contrast, the
French in Indochina and Algeria did not come to this
realization.

Several British governments put this principle into
practice with considerable style and grace. Splendid
flag-lowering ceremonies, handshakes, good wishes
and sentimental band concerts marked the British
surrender of their Empire. They acted like benign
parents sending off their adolescent children. In most
places, it was a good show, well carried off.

Like parents of adolescents sent off into the
world, the British hoped to maintain subtle ties with
their offspring. The Commonwealth of Nations has
been described as a body created to ameliorate the loss
of an empire. It is a vague, amorphous body, a shadow
of an international body, which engages in discussions
more than anything else.

Yet there is much more than the Commonwealth
to stand for the British heritage in that vast portion of
the globe once included in the Empire. Wherever English is spoken, at least something of British ideas of fair
play, public honesty, government by law and due process survive. Critics of imperialism notwithstanding,
British people have good reason for looking back upon

their Empire with pride. Of all the imperial peoples in history, from the Mongols and Romans to the Germans and Russians, the British were the mildest in their rule of subject peoples. Then, too, not having an empire any longer has been cushioned by the fact that the average Briton has been better off economically in the postwar years than ever before in history.

Swinging Britain: Postwar Affluence Arrives in a New Elizabethan Era

Many observers expected Europe to take decades to emerge from the ashes of World War II. This was not to be the case. The Continent bounded back with an amazing vitality, producing goods, services and babies in vast and unexpected quantities. Affluence came to Europe as it had come to the United States in the 1950s. Britain was somewhat behind West Germany, France and Italy, where wartime destruction necessitated starting from scratch with fresh plants and new techniques. Many of Britain's tired old industries used the same tired, old machines and techniques left over from before the war. Nevertheless, unprecedented affluence managed to reach Britain also by the 1960s.

Imagine what the late sixties and early seventies would have been for America without the war in Vietnam and the civil disturbance associated with it. Britain had all of the dynamic change and growth of the period without war abroad and without civil discord at home. The Conservative Prime Minister, Harold MacMillan, coined an apt phrase which stuck: "You never had it so good!" Indeed, it was true. The welfare state had raised the level of life and expectations for the poor, and a surge of economic and cultural achievement pushed the middle classes into the new lifestyle of abundance. For a while, it seemed that things would get better and better as time went on.

All Americans know something about this era in Britain because it was the time of the Beatles, the Rolling Stones and all of those exciting and strange fashions to come out of places like Carnaby Street before Carnaby Street became another tourist attraction. Who can forget the mini-skirt and one of its variations that appeared to be nothing more than a large belt? Everywhere it seemed that a new and youthful British culture was flowering. Britain was, in the realm of music and style at least, once again the center of the world.

In politics, there were no dramatic shifts in the sixties and seventies. Labour governments traded places with Conservative governments in the fifties, sixties and seventies without marked changes. Various Prime Ministers — Eden, MacMillan, Douglas-Home, Wilson, Heath and Callaghan — carried out relatively minor adjustments in a system that seemed to be working quite well.

Joining the EEC, or European Economic Community, or Common Market, became a very divisive issue by the early seventies. The Labour government joined in 1972 and held a referendum on the move in 1975. Although the referendum passed, controversy about EEC continues. Perhaps an advantage is greater cosmopolitanism in Britain; perhaps a disadvantage is a loss in insular pride.

A decided change in British political history did come in 1979 with the election of a Conservative government under Mrs. Thatcher that was pledged to reverse to some degree the economic and social arrangements which had been developed for over three decades.

Affluence in Doubt: The Late Seventies and the Eighties

The dream of a new, vibrant Elizabethan age was disturbed by some harsh economic realities. Inflation, competition from other countries, unemployment and recession interrupted this dream. By the mid-seventies many realized that chronic problems with too few exports and too many imports, inefficiency stemming from trade union regulations, and inflation from over-zealous government spending were not going away through the application of postwar techniques of economic management. Disposable incomes eroded and unemployment grew. Some began to fear a return to the gray grimness of the thirties, while others continued to see economic problems as temporary and correctable checks on the road to greater and greater prosperity for all. Yet others demanded a thoroughgoing socialism to replace the postwar mixed economy.

Whether the optimists or the pessimists, the socialists or the conservatives or the economic technocrats have a more realistic perspective on contemporary Britain certainly remains an open question. It is a very mixed picture. Strikes and protest movements mark continuing social unrest. On the bright side, one can still see much of the vitality and good living standards of the new Elizabethan era continuing. After all, rich Arabs throng to London to spend their oil millions in one of the best places in the world to acquire a wide variety of excellent consumer goods. Youth has picked up some new and, for some, disturbing cultural stimuli in the "punk" and "new wave" movements. Regardless of whether one sees these new adventures in music and color as fun or frightful, they are done with British style.

INDEX